Heidegger's Philosophy

HEIDEGGER'S *Philosophy*

A GUIDE TO HIS BASIC THOUGHT

Magda King

The Macmillan Company, New York
Collier-Macmillan Limited, London

First Printing

Acknowledgment of copyrighted material appears on page vii.

The Macmillan Company, New York
Collier-Macmillan Canada Ltd., Toronto, Ontario

Library of Congress catalog card no.: 64–12532

Printed in the United States of America

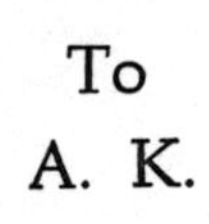

To

A. K.

ACKNOWLEDGMENTS

I wish to thank the Niemeyer Verlag for kind permission to quote and translate passages from the original edition of *Sein und Zeit,* copyright by Max Niemeyer Verlag, Halle/Saale (now Tübingen), 1927.

The manuscript has greatly benefited from my husband's advice and fruitful criticism; to him I owe deepest gratitude. I gladly take this opportunity also to thank George Kay for his most generous and constructive help through many years; and Thorir Thordarson and Martin Gray for their encouragement and support. Finally, I should like to thank The Macmillan Company for their unfailing courtesy and help in preparing this book for publication.

CONTENTS

BIBLIOGRAPHY

(Abbreviations of titles in the left-hand column are used in references)

HEIDEGGER

SZ	*Sein und Zeit*. Jahrbuch für Philosophie und phänomenologische Forschung, VIII. Halle: Niemeyer, 1927.
KANT	*Kant und das Problem der Metaphysik*. Frankfurt: Klostermann, 1951.
GRUND	*Vom Wesen des Grundes*. Frankfurt: Klostermann, 1955.
MET	*Was ist Metaphysik?* Mit Einleitung und Nachwort. Frankfurt: Klostermann, 1955.
WW	*Vom Wesen der Wahrheit*. Frankfurt: Klostermann, 1954.
EM	*Einführung in die Metaphysik*. Tübingen: Niemeyer, 1953.
	Platons Lehre von der Wahrheit. Mit einem
HU	*Brief über den "Humanismus."* Bern: Francke, 1947.
HO	*Holzwege*. Frankfurt: Klostermann, 1950.
	Erläuterungen zu Hölderlins Dichtung. Frankfurt: Klostermann, 1951.
DENKEN	*Was heisst Denken?* Tübingen: Niemeyer, 1954.
V/A	*Vorträge und Aufsätze*. Pfullingen: Neske, 1954.
	Aus der Erfahrung des Denkens. Pfullingen: Neske, 1954.
	Was ist das—die Philosophie? Pfullingen: Neske, 1956.
	Zur Seinsfrage. Frankfurt: Klostermann, 1956.
	Der Satz vom Grund. Pfullingen: Neske, 1958.
ID	*Identität und Differenz*. Pfullingen: Neske, 1957.
GE	*Gelassenheit*. Pfullingen: Neske, 1959.
US	*Unterwegs zur Sprache*. Pfullingen: Neske, 1960.

HUSSERL

Logische Untersuchungen. Halle: Niemeyer, 1913 (Bd. 1), 1921 (Bd. 2).

IDEEN I & II — *Ideen zu einer reinen Phänomenologie und phänomenologischen Philosophie*. 1. 2. & 3. Buch. *Husserliana*. Haag: Nijhoff, 1950 (Bd. 3), 1952 (Bd. 4 & Bd. 5).

Cartesianische Meditationen und Pariser Vorträge. *Husserliana*, Bd. 1. Haag: Nijhoff, 1950.

Vorlesungen zur Phänomenologie des inneren Zeitbewusstseins. Hgg. v. M. Heidegger. Jahrbuch für Philosophie und phänomenologische Forschung, IX. Halle: Niemeyer, 1928.

Foreword

The studies contained in this volume are intended to help the reader toward an understanding of Heidegger's philosophy, especially as it is expressed in *Sein und Zeit*. The translation of this treatise, published in 1962, has for the first time made Heidegger accessible to the English-speaking public.* Many of his later works, it is true, have been available in English for a longer time, but they remained a body without a head until *Sein und Zeit* had been translated. The possibility now opened up for a study of Heidegger's philosophy makes the need for expository works more urgent than before. Even the best translations cannot avoid a certain distortion of the original text, imposing additional difficulties on their readers. The main purpose of this book is to help such readers over the greatest initial difficulties presented by *Sein und Zeit*.

Several introductory and expository works on Heidegger have already appeared in English. Those that are known to

* *Being and Time,* trans. J. Macquarrie and E. Robinson (London: SCM Press, and New York: Harper & Row, 1962).

me vary greatly in seriousness and merit, but all seem to have one fault in common: they fail to bring fully to light the question Heidegger asks. It is not surprising, therefore, that Heidegger's answer is often misunderstood, or, what is worse, only half-understood. This state of affairs is admittedly easier to point out than to remedy. Heidegger claims to have made a new departure in Greek-Western thinking by raising a radically new problem. What this problem is, and how it differs from the central problem of traditional philosophy, is hard to grasp and harder to explain; but it must be at least roughly explained and understood before any detail of Heidegger's thought can fall into place.

Accordingly, the first theme of this book is simply the question Heidegger *asks*. The discussion of this question will at the same time introduce the reader to *Sein und Zeit* in a general way and prepare him for the second and main theme of this book: an exposition of those features and problems of *Sein und Zeit* which are both basic to its understanding and are usually found hardest to grasp, such as, to mention only one example, Heidegger's conception of world. The first seven studies will deal with problems basic to *Sein und Zeit* as a whole, the eighth will give a preview of the special problems raised in Division Two, and the concluding study will attempt to indicate Heidegger's answer to the question raised at the beginning of his inquiry.

The difficulty of Heidegger's thought was for many years held to be almost insuperable in the medium of a foreign language, especially English. That this opinion is no longer so widely held can be seen both from the rapidly increasing translations of Heidegger's works and from the interest of a growing public. There are signs, moreover, that as a thinker of our own age, Heidegger may be of interest to many who do not claim to have a wide knowledge of traditional metaphysics or whose concern with him may not be primarily philosophical at all. Such readers have a certain advantage in bringing an open mind to a new problem, but they also have special difficulties in grappling with Heidegger. Every effort has been made to carry these readers along in this work. Wherever possible, difficult ideas are approached through concrete examples and illustrations. Care has been taken to explain frequently used metaphysical terms, which are elementary to the expert in philosophy, but may be unfamiliar to the less well-prepared reader. Any unnecessary use of technical language has been avoided and a simple, straightforward English aimed at.

Heidegger's own key words present a special problem to translator and expositor alike, a problem that can never be entirely satisfactorily or finally solved. As Heidegger rightly insists, every translation is in itself an interpretation. The English renderings of key concepts which this work gives have grown entirely from its own understanding of Heidegger's thought, and may considerably differ from other translations. The first English version of *Sein und Zeit* appeared only after the body of this book had been completed, but as even a hasty comparison shows, there are many similarities and many more divergencies in the rendering of Heidegger's key words. This is all to the good. Since in most cases the English expression can only be an approximation to the German, it unavoidably weights the original in one way or another. Something like a standard English terminology of Heidegger's concepts is not only an impracticable aim, but would in advance rob his thought of its rich possibilities and drive it into the narrow channel of only one possible interpretation. For this reason, no effort was made to adapt the terminology of this book to that of *Being and Time,* except where the translators have found an especially felicitous way of expressing what seems to me the primary meaning of a word, as for instance, in their inspired translation of *eigenst* by "ownmost." This and several other excellent renderings have been gratefully taken over, and the term "Division" for *Abschnitt* has also been adopted.

An exposition has the advantage of far greater freedom than is permissible to a translation; it can not only paraphrase and expound a concept at length, where necessary, but it is one of its positive tasks to unfold all the implications enclosed in a key concept. Even so, when all this has been done, the inadequacy of the English rendering is often still so painfully felt that there is a constant temptation to go on using the German original. This temptation will be rigorously resisted in this work, on the principle that an inadequate English word is preferable to an unfamiliar foreign word, always provided that it has been carefully explained how and where the English fails to harmonize with the original. Only the titles of Heidegger's works will be kept in German. When *Being and Time* is used instead of *Sein und Zeit,* the reference is always to the English translation.

Heidegger's practice of putting into quotation marks, for no apparent reason, such familiar words as "subject," "know," "world," etc., although a minor difficulty, cannot be entirely disregarded. The quotation marks indicate that these words are not to be taken at their face value, either because they are used in a new sense, or because they are a loose way of speaking, not strictly appropriate to the matter under discussion, but unavoidable because they have grown from a long habit of thought and are easily understandable to the reader.

Heidegger's practice will be applied in this book only within strict limits. On the other hand, quotation marks will occasionally be used for purely linguistic reasons. The word *being,* when it stands for the substantive *das Sein,* may sometimes have to be distinguished from a gerund or a present participle that belongs to the sentence construction. English is exceptional in that it does not have a noun form of the infinitive *to be,* a peculiarity that can lead to confusion and obscurity when the *to be* is the main theme of the inquiry. Many philosophical works try to overcome this difficulty by spelling the gerund with a capital letter: Being. This practice, unfortunately, can lead to another confusion: the mere sight of the word *Being* suggests the divine Being, when what is meant is simply the humble *to be.* The verbal noun *being* will therefore be spelled with the small initial letter, but it will stand in quotation marks when any doubt could arise about its meaning.

Finally, two closely connected points must be briefly mentioned. The first concerns the Bibliography on pages xiii–xiv. It lists only those works on which this book is directly based, or which have contributed to it in a positive way. Two important new works by Heidegger were published when the manuscript was already too far advanced to be able to profit from them, and they have accordingly been omitted from the Heidegger bibliography. Among Husserl's many works, those have been selected to which either direct reference is made or which were found to be especially helpful as a preparation for *Sein und Zeit.* As to commentaries and critical works on Heidegger, none is included in the Bibliography, for the simple reason that none was drawn upon. To have considered the secondary literature that has grown up around Heidegger would almost inevitably have raised controversy and interfered with the main purpose of taking the reader directly to Heidegger's thought as that is presented in his own works.

For similar reasons, no attempt has been made at a critical appraisal of Heidegger's philosophy. Where comparisons with other thinkers occur, these are incidental and subordinate to the positive task of helping the reader to a clear and firm grasp of Heidegger's fundamental ideas. This is by no means easy, but once it is done, it will put the reader in a position both to explore more deeply Heidegger's thought for himself and to form a fair judgment of its power and original contribution to philosophy.*

* The question of a fruitful critique of Heidegger will be discussed at the end of a detailed study of Division Two of *Sein und Zeit*, by which the writer intends to follow up the present general exposition of this basic work.

Heidegger's Philosophy

PART ONE

What Is the Question?

Introductory

The main body of *Sein und Zeit* is preceded by two expository chapters in which Heidegger explains the question of being as it is to be raised and worked out in this fundamental inquiry. Everything that belongs to Heidegger's question, its motive and aim, the method of the investigation and the conclusions at which it will arrive, is set out in these two chapters with meticulous care and a masterliness that can only be appreciated after much study. And yet, twenty and thirty years after the publication of *Sein und Zeit,* Heidegger still finds himself obliged to correct misinterpretations of his fundamental work and to point out confusions between his question of being and that raised by traditional ontology.*

* The word "ontology" is used throughout this book in the sense defined by Heidegger: it is the inquiry into *beings as beings.* This inquiry considers beings purely in what and how they are, i.e. in respect of their being. Hence a second definition of ontology, namely as the inquiry into the *being of beings,* is often used by Heidegger as equivalent to the definition given first. Ontology, theology, logic, in their essential unity, constitute metaphysics as a whole. For a discussion of the threefold unity of metaphysics, see e.g. Heidegger's lecture, "Die onto-theo-logische Verfassung der Metaphysik," ID, p. 37 ff. (A list of the abbreviations of titles used in references is given in the Bibliography, cf. pp. xiii–xiv.)

The difficulty of grasping a radically new problem is, of course, well known to students of philosophy. In addition, Heidegger presents his readers with unusual difficulties, the greatest of which is the fragmentary state of *Sein und Zeit* itself. Divisions One and Two of Part I were published in 1927 as the beginning of a much larger work, consisting of two parts or halves, each containing three divisions. Heidegger intended to conclude his own investigations of the problem of being in Division Three, Part I, while the whole of Part II was to have been a radical critique of traditional ontology. Of this monumental work, the originally published two divisions are still all we have up to the present time. Perhaps nothing can show the stature of *Sein und Zeit* more impressively than the fact that, in spite of its unfinished state, it is one of those rare works whose importance can in no way be measured or foreseen.

Between 1927 and 1960, Heidegger published numerous other works, some of which clearly belonged to Part II of *Sein und Zeit* (see especially *Kant und das Problem der Metaphysik*). On the whole, it may be said that, except for a treatise on Aristotle's interpretation of time, the ground assigned to Part II has been fully covered by Heidegger, although not in the way in which it had been originally planned. In the Preface to the seventh German edition of *Sein und Zeit* (1953), Heidegger announced that the second half would definitely not be added to the work.

This announcement still left open the question of the crucially important Division Three of Part I, which was to have borne the suggestive subtitle of "Zeit und Sein" (Time and Being). The absence of this division has contributed more than any other single factor to the difficulty of the whole treatise. As far as one can judge, it was to have brought not only the solution of Heidegger's final problem, but also the explicit and detailed answer to what might be called his penultimate question. The absence of two sets of answers from *Sein und Zeit* makes its central problem extremely difficult to grasp and even leaves it open to doubt which of the questions raised by Heidegger is the more fundamental.

In 1961, however, Heidegger delivered a lecture on "Zeit und Sein" (Time and Being) at the University of Kiel, which was subsequently broadcast in Germany. The text of the lecture has unfortunately not yet become available outside Germany. It remains to be seen what light it will throw on Division Three and how it will contribute to an understanding of the work as a whole. Until its publication, an exposition of *Sein und Zeit* needs must restrict itself to Divisions One and Two as they stand in the treatise at present.

It need hardly be pointed out that even if Heidegger's fundamental work were completed, it would still be hard to approach, and great efforts would always be demanded from the reader to grasp its central theme. Among its many difficulties, the following may be specially mentioned:

First, the special use of the word *Sinn* (sense, or meaning), which enters importantly into Heidegger's problem as it is formulated in *Sein und Zeit*. This word is confusing and even positively misleading to readers who are unfamiliar with phenomenology. This difficulty, however, is comparatively easy to overcome.

Second, the confusion between Heidegger's and the metaphysical question of being. This difficulty is recurrent and not at all easy to overcome.

Third, the failure to see that there is any difficulty at all. Our familiarity with, and constant use of, the *is* and *am* and *to be,* make it incomprehensible that anyone should find our ability to understand these words astonishing and problematic. This difficulty is chronic and hardest to overcome, because it is not primarily a matter of intellect and thinking. A. E. Housman is reported to have said that the only way in which he could recognize great poetry was by a certain feeling in his stomach; it might equally well be said that the first time one truly understands Heidegger's questions one knows it by a cold shiver running down one's spine.

These difficulties will be specially kept in view in the exposition of Heidegger's central theme, which will be developed as follows:

In *Sections 1 and* 2 the precise meaning of Heidegger's question is explained and illuminated by a discussion of the aims set in Part I of *Sein und Zeit.*

Section 3. A brief summary is given of Heidegger's interpretation of the question of being as it has been asked and worked out in traditional philosophy, in contrast to his own question.

Section 4. The unique nature of the concept of being, and the attempted solutions of the problem of its unity, most notably by Aristotle, are discussed. This leads to a consideration of Heidegger's own attempt to solve the same problem.

Section 5. The concrete working out of Heidegger's problem in *Sein und Zeit* is the main subject. The difficulties inherent in the problem itself are discussed, concluding with a brief indication of the place of *Sein und Zeit* in Heidegger's thought as a whole.

⸙ Exposition

1. *A formal statement of the question*

Sein und Zeit is an inquiry into the *meaning of being (Sinn von Sein)*. To this short formulation of his theme, Heidegger frequently adds the word *überhaupt,* which is difficult to translate precisely: the meaning of being *as such* or *in general* is only an approximate statement of the full theme *(Sinn von Sein überhaupt)*. Fortunately, this difficulty need not worry us unduly, since Heidegger does not insist on a single formula. In an effort to make his problem concretely understandable, he often reduces it to a simple, informal question, as, for example: *"—was heisst 'Sein—.'"* (Cf. SZ, p. 26; also Kant, p. 202; ID, p. 21.) Almost literally translated, the phrase means: what is called "being"? Freely paraphrased, it might be rendered as: what do we mean by "to be"?

From these various formulations, the core of Heidegger's question emerges with an apparent, not to say misleading, clarity and simplicity. At first sight, we must confess, it is frankly disappointing. Heidegger claims to give philosophy a new start, but it is not at all evident where the newness of his question lies. It strikes us rather as the revival of an old question that has gone out of fashion. Even less does its fundamental character show itself on the surface. It reminds us of the kind of problems that are usually dealt with by logic, but most of all it sounds like a linguistic or a merely verbal problem. Among all the doubts and misgivings aroused by a formal statement of Heidegger's theme, the suspicion that he might be concerned merely with the meaning of a word must evidently be the first to be allayed.

2. *A provisional explanation of "meaning"* (Sinn). *The theme of* Sein und Zeit *restated*

Heidegger's special use of the term "meaning" (*Sinn*) was pointed out already in our introductory remarks. Our present difficulty thus seems to be purely terminological and should be capable of an easy solution: we must simply find out how Heidegger defines the word "meaning." The matter, however, is not quite so simple, as can be readily seen when the definition is actually given: meaning, in Heidegger's sense, is that from which something is understandable as the thing it is. This definition, while perfectly correct, is for our purpose quite insufficient. Heidegger's terminology grows from a way of phenomenological thinking, which cannot be explained merely by defining words. Phenomenology will be made the subject of one of our later studies, but in the meantime we must find a rough-and-ready way to understand Heidegger's use of "meaning." This can be done by a concrete illustration.

Supposing in a strange town we ask what a certain building is, we may be told that it is a theater. With this explanation, the building has explicitly come to our understanding *as* a theater, i.e. *as* the thing it is. Supposing, however, that we are not familiar with theaters, we must take a further step and have explained to us what a theater is. We shall be told that it is a building intended for the production of plays. Provided that we know at all what a play is, this particular building has now become manifest in what it essentially is. When we understand something *as* the thing it is, we have understood it in its *essential being.*

But where in all this is the meaning? Is it in our understanding of the word *theater*? No. Is it in this concrete thing, the theater itself? No. Is it perhaps in the explanation: "for the production of plays"? The "for" shows that this thing, the theater, is in advance understood by reference to a purpose; is that where we find the meaning? This comes much nearer to Heidegger, but is not quite there yet. Meaning, according to Heidegger, is that *from* which something is understandable as the thing it is. From where can a thing like a theater be understood at all? Only from a world of human existence. Writing, producing and appreciating plays is one of our distinctively human possibilities, for the sake of which we have things like theaters. Only from a human world can a thing be understood *as* a theater. That which makes such understanding possible, Heidegger says, is the meaning. The meaning of the theater is the world to which it belongs.

The world of our own existence is the horizon in which our everyday understanding moves, so that from it and in reference to it the things we come across are intelligible to us *as* theaters, *as* buses, *as* knives and forks, in one word, *as* things that can be useful for some purpose. The horizon of our world is primarily "meaning-giving"; it is a meaning in which we constantly move as a matter of course, so that it usually remains implicit.

One way to make this implied meaning explicit is to turn away from our everyday world and enter into the realm of one of the sciences, say, theoretical physics. At one stroke, things like theaters, buses, knives and forks, become "meaningless." The horizon from which things are now understood is the substantiality of matter. Why has such a startling change taken place? Because the horizon, in which the physicist's understanding moves, has undergone a profound modification: the world of human existence has become modified into a theoretical conception of material nature, articulated into such categories or basic concepts as mass, motion, energy, etc. Since this horizon alone is "meaning-giving" for the physicist, anything whatever that falls under his observation must show itself and can only show itself as a complex motion of material bodies. This horizon gives nothing from which things could even be questioned as to their possible relevance to a purpose; their only possibility now is to show themselves in their material properties as moving bodies in a space-time continuum.

To sum up the results we have reached so far: meaning is that which enables us to understand things *as* the things they are, i.e. in their essential being. The meaning does not originally lie in words, or in things, but in the remarkable structure of our understanding itself. We move in advance in a horizon of understanding, from which and in reference to which the things we meet are intelligible to us *as* so and so and *as* such and such. The world of our own existence is the horizon from which we primarily understand things *as* relevant to a purpose. This is capable of modifications, e.g. into something like "nature." From this horizon, things become understandable purely *as* substantial bodies. The modifications in the horizon of our understanding enable us to understand things in different ways, but in each case only in one or another of their possibilities.

What light does this throw onto Heidegger's theme? What is Heidegger aiming at when he asks: How is it at all possible for man to understand being? From what horizon does he understand being? What does being mean? These questions, as our discussion has shown, are not three different questions, but are one and the same. The horizon which makes it possible for us to understand being *as* being, is itself the meaning of being. What is this horizon? It is, as *Sein und Zeit* sets out to show, time. Already on the first page, Heidegger tells us that the provisional aim of his treatise is the interpretation of *time* as the possible horizon of any understanding whatever of being.

Why does Heidegger call this interpretation his *provisional* aim? Presumably to indicate that with its achievement, the tasks set to *Sein und Zeit* as a whole are by no means finished. Heidegger's interpretation of time is completed in Division Two, except for the last crucial steps, and these were to have been taken at the beginning of Division Three. This was to have led to the final phase of Heidegger's original investigations: the temporal interpretation of the idea of being as such.

In the absence of Division Three, this final aim of Part I of *Sein und Zeit* would have remained impenetrably obscure, had Heidegger not given some illuminating hints in his work entitled *Vom Wesen des Grundes,* published in 1929. Here Heidegger clearly indicates that the idea of being as such is to be articulated into what- and how-being, something, nothing and notness. (*Was- und Wiesein, Etwas, Nichts und Nichtigkeit,* cf. Grund, p. 52.)

This formula, bare as it is, and uncertain as its interpretation must be, yet helps to define Heidegger's central theme and deserves to be carefully considered. It contains, in fact, the basic design of the new ontology that is to be founded, i.e., brought back to its source-ground, in *Sein und Zeit*. The strangeness of Heidegger's philosophical approach makes itself felt already in the concepts into which the idea of being is articulated, among which the "nothing" and the "not" occupy the most important place. This seems paradoxical indeed, for, to our usual way of thinking, "nothing" and "notness" are the very opposite of being. Our later studies will show, however, that these concepts receive an entirely new interpretation in Heidegger's thought, in the light of which their central philosophical importance will become fully understandable. In the meantime, we shall turn to those articulations of the idea of being which seem familiar and more within our immediate grasp.

The two closely connected articulations of what- and how-being become much easier to comprehend when they are rephrased into what-(a thing)-is and how-(it)-is. The being of things is manifest to us in *what* they are, traditionally called the *essence,* and in *how* they are, i.e. whether they exist actually, or possibly, or necessarily. It should be noted, however, that these traditional conceptions should never be taken over unexamined and mechanically applied to Heidegger's philosophy. The reason for this will gradually emerge in the course of our studies; meantime, a more urgent point to decide is what we are to understand by the "thing" whose being is articulated into what and how.

In the primary and narrow sense, things are the concrete things that are accessible to us through the senses and are capable of an independent existence, such as mountains, stars, plants, animals, etc. These things stand there, so to speak, on their own feet, and in so standing, they are, they exist. Things in a very wide sense, however, can mean anything at all: beings as such and as a whole, and things in this wide sense constitute the sphere of philosophical inquiry. Within the realm of beings as a whole, however, the concrete, sensible things have played an eminently important part, so that non-sensible phenomena, like mind, knowledge, number, etc., have tended to be understood in comparison with and in contrast to them. In other words, the reality (*Wirklichkeit*) of one kind of thing has tended to be measured by the reality of another kind of thing.

But if the fundamental problem of philosophy is to be raised in a new way, not only the idea of being but also the idea of beings must be reconsidered and defined. The third articulation of the idea of being gives us the widest possible concept of beings as such: they are something and not nothing. A delusion, the meaning of a poem, God, hope, thinking, seeming, becoming, etc., are evidently something and not nothing, although they are not concrete, sensible things in the primary sense of the word. Starting from the idea of something, a "real thing" is no longer played off against an "ideal thing" and the one measured by the other; both are set off against the nothing as the totally other to all things, and understood in their most fundamental character as "not nothing." Heidegger's idea of being formulates the demand that ontology must start from the widest and deepest of all distinctions: the difference between something and nothing. With this start, the problem of the nothing would be drawn into the very center of philosophy; and this, Heidegger maintains, would be the first fruitful step toward "overcoming nihilism." (Cf. EM, p. 155.)

All this sounds intolerably paradoxical at present, because we do not in the least know as yet what Heidegger means by the nothing. For the same reason, it is hard to imagine that the nothing and the not can have anything to do with time, and yet they must have, if Heidegger is serious in announcing that the final aim of *Sein und Zeit* is to unfold the temporal meaning enclosed in the idea of being as such.

This culminating point of Heidegger's investigations will unfortunately remain obscure even at the end of our studies, since the whole temporal analysis of the idea of being was to have been carried out in Division Three. But, it will be asked, what of all the works Heidegger has written since *Sein und Zeit*? Is it possible that none of them brings at least a partial solution of Heidegger's final problem? One of them does, the *Einführung in die Metaphysik*. The lecture, delivered in 1935, on which this book is based, has rightly been felt to be unique among all Heidegger's works. Its true theme, however, has often been only imperfectly understood. It brings, it is true, the temporal interpretation of an idea of being, but not of Heidegger's own idea. The interpretation given is of a restricted conception of being which has been central to metaphysical thinking: the idea of substantial being.

What is the temporal meaning hidden in the idea of substantiality? Heidegger formulates it as "standing presentness" or "persistent presentness" (*ständige Anwesenheit*, cf. EM, p. 154). This is the horizon into which traditional philosophy, unknown to itself, looks out in advance, and in view to which it determines, differently in different ages, what kind of things have "true being" and which are in comparison mere shadows. It is not an accident, for instance, that Greek-Western thinking has ascribed an extraordinary dignity to the formal sciences like logic and mathematics. The purely formal concepts and their relations studied by these sciences preeminently satisfy the idea of permanence and unchanging presence, which is the temporal meaning of substantiality. (Cf. SZ, pp. 89 ff. esp. pp. 95–96.) The fact that the modern mathematical-theoretical sciences have grown from the soil of Greek-Western philosophy, and from no other soil, testifies to the hidden power of an idea of being which has carried and shaped the course of our history. But the possibilities of this idea have now been worked out. If the question of being has to be asked anew, this cannot be a mere whim or even a "stroke of genius" on the part of an individual; it can only arise from historical necessity.

How is this question to be worked out in *Sein und Zeit*?

The main stages can now be roughly delimited: The ultimate goal, as was shown above, is the temporal interpretation of the idea of being as such, i.e. of what- and how-being, something, nothing and notness. (Projected for Division Three.) This aim requires for its indispensable basis the solution of a provisional or penultimate problem: How is it at all possible for man to understand being? How is it that *time* is the horizon from which being is understandable? How is time itself to be interpreted? (Completed in Division Two, except for last crucial steps, which were to have been taken at the beginning of Division Three.) This problem, in turn, requires for its indispensable basis a preliminary inquiry into the being of man. The task of this investigation is to discover all the essential structures of man's existence, thereby illuminating the way in which man understands both his own being and the being of other beings. (Completed in Division One.)

Having brought the broad outline of Heidegger's treatise into focus, we can now summarize his question as follows: it is the question of the inner possibility of our understanding of being and of the temporal meaning enclosed in the idea of being as such. This is what Heidegger often calls the question of *being as being,* but the phrase is misleading, because the central problem of traditional ontology is usually defined in the same way. In view of the radical difference between the two, would it be justified to change the definition of traditional ontology to the one proposed by Heidegger? Is Heidegger's claim that he is providing a *fundamental* ontology, i.e. the foundation for all ontology, to be upheld? The problem of our understanding of being, Heidegger maintains, lies already in all the questions philosophy can ask, and lies in them in such a way that it cannot even be raised as a problem, let alone be solved, on the traditional soil. On what grounds does Heidegger put forward such a thesis? Is there sufficient evidence to make the thesis tenable, or should it be rejected as a dogmatic assertion? These matters demand an examination of traditional philosophy, whose nature and limits have so far been only briefly indicated.

3. *Why has traditional ontology failed to get to the root of the problem of being?*

The character and limits of Western philosophy are decisively determined by its Greek origins. The early Greek thinkers asked: What are beings as beings? What are beings as a whole? In spite of many profound changes in the course of Greek-Western thinking, the questions it asks are still fundamentally the same as they were at the beginning, or are derivations from them. Traditional ontology, Heidegger maintains, was and remains an inquiry into beings as beings, and not into being as such.

Beings * is a rendering of the German word *das Seiende.* This is Heidegger's translation of the essentially ambiguous Greek expression *to on,* which can mean both being and beings (*ta onta*). Since in Heidegger's translation the weight falls on the latter, it usually will be rendered by *beings,* and sometimes also by *things.* There are other ways, in themselves better and clearer, of translating *das Seiende,* e.g. the existent, the entity or entities. These translations are avoided here just because they are clearer: they cover over an ambiguity which Heidegger holds to be the very essence of metaphysical thinking. Phrases like "the being of the existent," or "the being of entities," have a first-blush understandability which is entirely spurious: they hide the problem which the phrase

* When the explanation of a key word has an essential bearing on Heidegger's thought, it will be given in the main text, unless it would interfere with the movement of an important passage. Purely technical remarks will be dropped into footnotes.

"the being of beings" wears, so to speak, on its sleeve.

Ta onta means: that which is, the things that are. Formally, the word "beings" approximates quite well to *ta onta,* but in English it is applied mainly to living beings, and primarily to human beings. We must now try to think this word in exactly the opposite way, because the beings par excellence which traditional ontology has in view are not the beings we ourselves are, but primarily things, in the sense of concrete, sensible things. When Greek-Western philosophy speaks of *to be,* it thinks of the *is* of a thing; in other words, *to be* has come to mean predominantly the infinitive of *is.* (Cf. EM, p. 70.)

What do we mean when we say that a thing *is* (exists)? We mean that it is really there among the all of things, that it occurs, it can be found somewhere in the natural universe. When we talk of reality, we mean primarily the actual presence of something among the totality of beings. The reality of the *res* (thing) in a very wide sense may be called the central conception of being in traditional ontology. The basic character of reality is substantiality. The seemingly irreconcilable trends in our philosophical tradition spring mainly from varying interpretations of what is meant by substance or what manner or class of beings may properly be called substances.* In ancient philosophy alone, substance has been as variously defined as matter, as material bodies, as essence, as number, as idea or form, as the indissoluble unity of matter and form, not to speak of modern variations on the same theme. Yet all these differences can be differentiated and all these opposites op-

* The fundamental changes *within* metaphysical thinking would naturally be given far more weight in a detailed discussion than can be done in this short sketch. For example, in the Latin word *substantia* there lies already a profound reinterpretation of the Greek idea of being as *ousia.* The term *substance,* according to Heidegger, is thoroughly inappropriate to Greek thought. At this stage, however, it is unavoidable to use a language that is familiar to the reader from the best known translations of Greek thinkers.

posed only on the ground of an underlying sameness: an idea of being as substantial reality.

No matter how variously traditional ontology may define the substance, it always does so with a view to self-subsistence, self-maintenance without recourse to other beings, unchanging presence as an independent self. And just because independence and self-subsistence are the basic characters of substantial being, its perfect embodiment must be self-produced, or unproduced, uncaused, uncreated. Anything that is brought into being is necessarily dependent, needs maintenance and is liable to pass away—that is why perishable, finite beings cannot satisfy the idea of the perfect substance.

Any problem that arises in traditional ontology is in advance understood in the horizon of substantiality. But this idea of being, Heidegger maintains, is too narrow and restricted to be able to explain all the ways and senses in which we can understand being. Above all, it is incapable of explaining the distinctively and uniquely human way of being. Man exists so that his being is *manifest* to him, and it is manifest to him as his own. That is why each of us must say of himself: I am. *Sein und Zeit* will show that the whole meaning and structure of the being we express by the *am* is totally different from the real existence of a thing.

Once we begin to think about it, it must strike us as curious that the infinitive *to be* should have primarily drawn its meaning from the *is* of things, when the *am* would seem to be much nearer and more easily comprehensible to us. Does Heidegger ascribe this strange feature of our tradition to a lack of insight or deep thought on the part of metaphysical thinkers? Far from it: he holds that the greatness of their thought has been the distinction of Europe. Was, then, the question: what are beings as beings? simply a wrong start, accidentally made and perpetuated through two and a half thousand years? Historical decisions, Heidegger maintains, do not come about by accident, but spring from the basic possibilities of man's existence, possibilities that are neither made by man, nor, on the other hand, are merely blindly and passively endured by him, as a thing may be thought to "endure" the contingencies that happen to it.

The tendency to interpret man's being from the being of things may be roughly and provisionally explained by one of the basic ways in which man can and usually does exist: he loses himself to the things he meets in his world. Owing to his fundamental tendency to give himself away, to scatter himself among his makings and doings, man literally finds himself "there," among the things with which he is busy. Hence the impression arises that *to be* means *I am* in exactly the same way as it does when it is applied to a thing. Thus the *to be* remains undifferentiated and is applied in the vague, average sense of presentness and occurrence to any beings that are accessible at all, including man himself.

It is from this average understanding of being that metaphysics grows. The horizon from which being is understood does not become explicit and its possible differentiations cannot become even a problem. What is differentiated is not being, but beings. Traditional philosophical distinctions start from beings, defining and dividing them into regions and classes according to their essence, their whatness. Man himself is enrolled into the region of living beings, of animals, among which, ontologically speaking, he subsequently remains. (Cf. Hu, pp. 65 ff.) Man is the animal who speaks, who has a soul, reason, mind, spirit, self-consciousness, who can think. The interpretation of man's essence undergoes many changes in Greek-Western ontology; what does not change is that man's existence is in advance understood as the real occurrence of a peculiar species among the all of beings.

But, it may be objected, Heidegger's interpretation of the history of Greek-Western philosophy is surely too extreme and one-sided. It may apply to ancient ontology, but it seems to leave out of account the influence of Christian theology on a considerable period of Western thought. There is a fundamental difference between the medieval and the Greek interpretation of man. And when we come to the modern era, has Descartes not radically reversed the Greek start with his "I think therefore I am"?

Heidegger's answer to these objections may be briefly indicated as follows:

a) The idea of the transcendence of man, that man reaches out beyond sheer rationality, that he is more than merely an intelligent animal, undoubtedly has its roots in Christian anthropology. (Cf. SZ, p. 49.) But what is decisive for the question of being is that man's *existence* never becomes an ontological problem. In Christian theology, man has a preeminent place among all other beings by virtue of a soul to be saved, but his existence is sufficiently explained by his being an *ens creatum,* a creature in a created world. For purely ontological problematics, the situation is not radically altered from the antique period: "to be created" is a Christian reinterpretation of "to be brought forth," which is a basic character of being already in Greek ontology.

b) In spite of the far-reaching change introduced into philosophy by Descartes, Heidegger repudiates the claim that a fundamentally new start is made with the "I think therefore I am." (Cf. SZ, pp. 89 ff.) Descartes uncritically takes over the medieval conception of being as the substantiality of substance. He follows the Scholastic division of substances into the infinite and finite substance, the *ens increatum* and the *ens creatum.* Far from raising the question of being in a radically new way, Descartes does not even attempt to get to the root of the meaning enfolded in the idea of substantiality, nor does it occur to him to ask whether the being of God or of man can be appropriately determined by this idea.

The philosopher's God, as Heidegger frequently points out, is totally different from the God revealed in religious experience. (Cf. ID, p. 70; Met, Einleitung, p. 20.) God as the uncreated being is a purely ontological concept. It is the perfect embodiment of what is explicitly or implicitly meant by substantiality: an uncaused, self-subsistent being that needs nothing apart from itself to remain constantly present as an unchanging self.

As against the most perfect, uncreated substance, created beings can only be called substances in a relative sense. Even among them, however, two regions can be distinguished that are relatively independent of production and maintenance: the *res cogitans* and the *res extensa,* the thinking thing and the extended thing. Descartes thus defines the essence of the created thing as extension on the one hand and as "I think" on the other hand. The "I am" is not only left unexamined, but is understood as a matter of course as the produced (created) presence of the thinking thing. Broadly and roughly speaking, "I think therefore I am" means: As the subject of the "I think," I am indubitably, necessarily present (as the absolutely unshakable ground of truth) in my representations.*

* Heidegger's interpretation of Descartes' *cogito sum* cannot be even approximately dealt with in this short sketch. It should be noted, however, that Heidegger is fully aware of the epochal change *within* metaphysical thinking that began with Descartes. The discussion of Descartes' "extended world" in the first Division of *Sein und Zeit* (chap. 3, B.) is misleading because of its incompleteness. At the time of writing, Heidegger intended to publish a full treatise on the *cogito sum* as the second Division of Part II of *Sein und Zeit.* Although Part II has not been and will not be published, Heidegger has repeatedly elucidated the meaning and importance of Descartes' principle in his later works (cf. especially Ho, pp. 80 ff. and pp. 91 ff.).

One of the besetting difficulties for the student of Heidegger's philosophy is to grasp that his interpretation of the being of man (*Dasein*) accomplishes

Far from making a new beginning with the problem of being, the modern age of science and technology brings to an unparalleled and extreme unfolding the implications that lie already in the Greek start. The extraordinary leveling down of everything to a uniform sameness witnessed by modern man in every sphere of experience is explained by Heidegger in the following way: In the latest stage of the modern era, even the object, with its last specific what-character of extension, disappears. Things no longer manifest their being by standing face to face with man as objects for a subject (*Gegenstand*), but by standing up to a thoroughgoing calculation, whereby their persistent availability and produceability is in advance made certain (*Bestand*). It is by no means an accident that logic and the mathematical-theoretical sciences, with their formal-symbolic, nonvisual representation of nature, now come to an unheard-of predominance: they are the executors of the idea of being as substantiality, which now reaches its apotheosis in reducing the what and how of things to the persistence of a characterless product, whose being lies solely in its calculable availability and disposability anywhere, at any time. (Cf. e.g. *Die Frage nach der Technik*, V/A, pp. 13 ff; also *ibid.*, p. 61; further Met, Nachwort, p. 48.) *

---

a radical break with the subjectivity of modern metaphysics, in spite of all appearances to the contrary. When Heidegger speaks of the "subject" in *Sein und Zeit,* he postulates that the whole idea of "being-a-subject," and with it, of "being-an-object," must be fundamentally re-thought and interpreted in the light of a new question of being.

* The main outline of Heidegger's interpretation of traditional philosophy is clearly discernible already in *Sein und Zeit,* and is amplified and expounded in many of his later works, for instance, in *Einführung in die Metaphysik; Was heisst Denken?; Identität und Differenz; Der Satz vom Grund,* etc.; also in numerous essays and lectures to be found in collections, e.g. *Holzwege* and *Vorträge und Aufsätze.*

4. *The uniqueness of the concept of being: the problem of its unity. Aristotle's "unity of analogy"—a lead into Heidegger's question*

The preceding discussions already indicate that logical methods of analysis and definition cannot be appropriate to the new inquiry into being. Logic has grown from the soil of traditional ontology; its methods, justifiable within certain limits, are applicable only to defining beings. (Cf. SZ, pp. 3–4.) But being is nothing like beings; it cannot be brought to definiteness and clarity by having beings ascribed to it. As Aristotle clearly saw, being is not the highest *genus*. The universality of the concept of being is of a totally different order from the generality of those concepts that gather beings into one class. While Aristotle's deep and subtle reasoning cannot be entered upon here, its point can be graphically illustrated: A *genus,* which through its subordinate species contains individual beings, can always be exemplified and thus brought to definiteness and clarity. The *genus* animal, for instance, can always be explained by pointing to a sheep or a horse. But to explain the concept of being, we should vainly point to a horse or a mountain or the sun, saying: "Look, that is what I mean by *is.*" The very absurdity of this attempt shows the baffling character of our most universal concept: while everything that we can know, feel, experience in any way is understandable to us in terms of its being, being itself can in no way be explained from or by beings. Its universality transcends, goes out beyond any possible beings or classes of beings.

The uniqueness of being gives rise to the important philosophical problem: what constitutes the unity of this universal concept? The unity of a *genus,* like *animal,* may be explained by the common character of the beings that fall under it, but this cannot be done with being. And yet, all the ways and senses in which we use the term *to be* have a recognizable and definite unity, and the philosophical task is to explain how this unity is possible.

This is the problem Aristotle tried to solve with his teaching of the analogous meanings of being. "With this discovery," Heidegger remarks on page 3 of *Sein und Zeit,* "Aristotle shifted . . . the problem of being onto a radically new basis." But even Aristotle, Heidegger goes on to point out, failed to solve the problem of those "categorial connections" which he himself had raised, nor could the medieval Schoolmen, who took over the doctrine of the unity of analogy, arrive at any solution in principle.

Why does Heidegger so pointedly draw attention to this doctrine in the opening pages of *Sein und Zeit*? What is it that Aristotle and the Schoolmen failed to solve? Why must the whole problem remain in principle insoluble within metaphysics itself? The answer to these questions must obviously throw a great deal of light, not only on traditional attempts, but on Heidegger's own attempt to grapple with the fundamental problems of philosophy. The whole matter, therefore, is well worth considering, even though we can do so only briefly and by way of illustrations.

The specific problem which the Schoolmen tried to solve was how it was possible to say "God is" and "the world is," when there is an infinite difference between the being of the Creator and of the created world. (Cf. SZ, p. 93.) Following Aristotle's teaching, the Schoolmen explained that the word "is" does not mean exactly the same in every instance. God *is* (exists) in the primary and full sense of the word *to be*. The world *is* only in a derivative sense, which is understood by analogy, i.e. by reference to the first and unqualified meaning of the term.

According to Aristotle, only "substance" *is* (exists) in the primary and independent sense of *to be*. Anything that belongs to a category other than substance, e.g. the category of quality, quantity, state, relation, etc., is said to be only in a qualified sense, being the quality, quantity, state, etc. of a substance. For example, the "concrete and unique substance," the moon, which Aristotle holds to be eternal and divine, *is* (exists) in the primary and full sense of the word *to be*. But when we say "The moon is white," or "The moon is eclipsed," the meaning of the *is* has been qualified. The difference between the substance moon and its quality of whiteness or its state of being eclipsed is evident: The whiteness could not exist by itself, whereas the moon could very well change its color and yet remain substantially the moon. Similarly, the eclipse has no separate existence apart from the moon, whereas the moon remains identically the same without being eclipsed. And yet, we do not speak ambiguously or improperly when we ascribe being of a kind to quality, or state, or quantity, etc., because in these instances we do not mean the same by the word *is* as when we speak of substance. We are using the term analogously, i.e. by reference to its first and unqualified meaning.

Why does Heidegger draw attention to the importance of the "unity of analogy" at the beginning of *Sein und Zeit*? Because here is the nearest approach that can be made from metaphysics toward a new inquiry into being. Aristotle sees clearly that the problem cannot be solved by dividing beings into genera and species, but that the "to be" itself must be articulable and modifiable. He sees further that the modifications can be explained by *reference* to a primary meaning. But even Aristotle's genius cannot leap out of an idea of being as being-a-substance, which determines traditional ontology from its start.

What is it, among other things, that the unity of analogy fails to illuminate? It fails to illuminate the *primary* meaning of being. How is it, Heidegger would ask, that "to be" must primarily mean "to-be-substance"? And why must substantiality mean self-subsistence, self-maintenance in unchanging identity? Are these basic characters of being the arbitrary invention of philosophers? Or have they, on the contrary, been "wrung from the phenomena themselves" in the highest efforts of thinking? If the latter is the case, as Heidegger holds it is, then the question must at last be asked: how is it possible for us to understand something like substantial-being at all? From where and in reference to what is this primary meaning of being understood? Self-subsistence, unchanging presence, persistence as an identical self—in all this there lies a distinct reference to time. Time is the horizon in which not only the traditional, but any understanding whatever of being in advance moves.

Until time is explicitly laid bare as that which makes our understanding of being *as* being possible, and until the original phenomenon of time itself is properly explained, the problem of the unity of being remains in principle insoluble. When, on the other hand, it has been shown that all possible differentiations, not merely of beings, but of the *to be* itself have indeed been drawn from time and can be explained as modifications of and derivations from time, then this ancient and troubling philosophical problem will have found a radical solution.

Traditional ontology draws its central idea of being from only one mode of time—the present, the now. The more persistently something is present, the more truly it *is*. "The philosopher's God," it can now be seen, most perfectly satisfies this idea of being: to be ever-present in unchanging self-sameness in an infinite succession of nows. By a curious reflex action, this idea of being is turned back upon the time from which it had been drawn: time itself is conceived as something that is, and its being is characterized as an infinite succession of now-points of which only each present now is "real." The past is conceived as a now that no longer is, the future as a now that is not yet. This interpretation of time has maintained itself from the Greek period down to our own day. It will be the task of *Sein und Zeit* to show that the *infinite* now-time, in which things come into being and pass away, while it is a genuine time-phenomenon, is not the *original* phenomenon of time.

Where and how does the now-time of our philosophical tradition become accessible? It is accessible in a preeminent presentation, which has of old been called *noein,* the pure, nonsensuous apprehending of the being of beings. This philosophical "seeing" presents to itself beings in respect of their pure presence. According to Heidegger, however, time is originally manifest to us not in what and how things are, but in our own being, the *I am,* and this time is *finite.* The finite time of our own existence, however, is too inexorable to disclose itself to a mere harmless "looking at it": it is elementally and originally disclosed in dread (*Angst*). The extraordinary importance of dread in *Sein und Zeit* does not make this work into an existentialistic *Angst-Philosophie;* the importance of dread lies in its ontological function of disclosure. The pure, nonsensuous apprehending, the *noein,* which has traditionally been regarded as the one proper approach to the being of beings, proves to be inadequate to the inquiry into being as being.

5. *How is the new inquiry into being to be concretely worked out? Difficulties arising from the nature of the problem itself*

Our discussions so far have had the aim of bringing the central problem of *Sein und Zeit* into focus. The solution proposed by Heidegger has to some extent been indicated, not in the hope of making it understandable at this stage, but in order to illuminate the fundamental nature of the problem itself and its departure from tradition. On the other hand, the way in which Heidegger works out his theme has so far been only briefly mentioned, and needs a somewhat fuller discussion.

The subtitles of the two divisions we have of *Sein und Zeit* seem to suggest that this work is an ontological inquiry of the usual style into the being of man. Division One is entitled: "The Preparatory Fundamental Analysis of the Being of Man"; Division Two: "The Being of Man and Time." * To all appearances, *Sein und Zeit* sets out to repair the omission of traditional ontology to inquire into man's existence and not only into his essence. If we follow the customary division of the all of beings into great ontological regions—the modern practice is to separate the region "nature" from the region "mind"—it seems perfectly appropriate to call *Sein und Zeit* a "regional ontology of man," or, to use an equivalent expression, to call it a "philosophical anthropology."

The only obstacle to such a reasonable interpretation is Heidegger's own, almost obstinate insistence that his treatise is not a regional but a fundamental ontology. (Cf. Kant, pp. 188 ff.) Its sole aim is to show how an understanding of being is at all possible, and why the being understood in it must have a temporal character. The inquiry into man's existence, Heidegger insists, is only the concrete *way* toward this aim. Why is this plain and unambiguous statement yet so puzzling? Basically, because it is by no means self-evident why Heidegger's sole aim should make an analysis of all the essential structures of man's being necessary. Why cast the net so widely to catch

* The translation of Heidegger's word *Zeitlichkeit* by "time" is a temporary expedient which will be corrected at the first opportunity. Similarly, the meaning of *Dasein* and the renderings adopted for it will be fully explained in the next part.

a single fish? To understand being, we are inclined to think, must surely belong to man's reason, or self-consciousness, or to whatever faculty of understanding he may be shown to possess. Why does Heidegger take such an apparently circuitous way for working out his problem?

Because, according to Heidegger, man's understanding of being is not an isolated faculty, nor merely a part of himself, but determines through and through his whole way of being: man's way to be is to understand. Man *is* so that in his concrete, factual existence his being is manifest to him as *I am.* This unique character of man, that he exists understandingly, is not confined merely to his thinking or cognitive activities, but a priori determines all the ways in which he can be; for instance, he cannot be even a body in the same way as a merely living organism. (Cf. Hu, p. 67.)

It is man's unique way of existing which metaphysical thinkers tried to explain by ascribing his understanding of being to his soul, or reason, or self-consciousness, or to whatever other interpretation of man's essence they may have given. With such interpretation, however, man is broken into two, if not three, layers, i.e. body, soul and spirit, so that an explanation of his being becomes well-nigh impossible. What should be the ontological character of this pieced-together man? Does he exist really, or ideally, or partly one way and partly another way? Man, Heidegger insists, cannot exist ideally, as a disembodied spirit, as a pure I, as an absolute consciousness, because, as we shall see later, his "thrownness" into a world a priori belongs to and helps to constitute his "spirituality." Nor, on the other hand, can man exist merely really like a stone, which is essentially hidden to itself in its being. Man's way to be is unique: it is as far removed from an ideal-being as it is from the real-being of a thing. Even the living-being of the highest animals is separated by an abyss from man's way of existing.

(Cf. Hu, p. 69.) Beings like plants and animals are not merely real like stones: their way to be is to live. But they are wholly dissolved in living, whereas man transcends, goes out beyond living, i.e. to him the finiteness of living is wholly disclosed, and this alone, as *Sein und Zeit* sets out to show, is what enables him to understand both himself and others in their being.

No animal, not even the highest, can treat a thing as the thing it is. This way of understanding things, as far as we know, is the unique distinction of man. But just because it is native to him, it usually remains unnoticed. In his ordinary, everyday existence, man lives in a "preontological," i.e. implicit, understanding of being as a matter of course. It seems the greatest commonplace to him that to the merest glance a thing like a tree, for instance, should present itself as something that *is*. He is usually too absorbed in his business with the tree itself to notice the remarkable fact that if the *is* were missing from the tree, not merely the word *is* would disappear, but also the tree *as* tree. He might, it is true, be still aware of it in some other way which is difficult for us even to imagine, but the tree could no longer present itself as the thing it is, in its specific tree-being. Consequently, there could be no such word as tree. If the *is* were missing from our language, there would be not a single other word and no language at all. (Cf. EM, p. 62.)

Since in his usual absorption in things, man constantly overlooks that which enables him to exist as man, his unique understanding of being, philosophy is needed to take being for its explicit and, according to Heidegger, its only proper theme. At the same time, philosophy can be nothing other than a radicalization of the vague, average understanding of being in which man always and already exists. "The secret judgments of the common understanding," and they alone, as

Kant said, are "the philosophers' business." (Quoted by Heidegger, SZ, p. 4, and frequently elsewhere.) Accordingly, Heidegger chooses just the ordinary, everyday manner of existence for the concrete basis of his "Preparatory Fundamental Analysis of the Being of Man." (Division One.) Its task is not only to show what is essentially, a priori constitutive of man's average manner of being, but at the same time to explain the elemental trend toward the world which characterizes everyday existence. Only when the self-disguise which lies in man's lostness to his world has been explicitly laid bare, can a more original and radical understanding of being be made accessible for investigation. (Division Two.)

Man's way to be is to understand being. This way of being is unique to man. Consequently, all possible articulations in the idea of being must come to light in the essential structures of man's existence, and it is only there that they can come to light. Once this is clearly seen, it becomes evident that in examining how the whole man is, and how he wholly is, Heidegger is far from taking a circuitous route to a distant goal. He is, in a sense, at the goal already with the first step, i.e. he is already examining the possibilities enclosed in the idea of being as such. On the other hand, it is true that in each of its phases the inquiry moves into a deeper ontological level, so that while the whole of *Sein und Zeit* makes up the fundamental ontology, it is only in Division Three that the fundamental ontology can come fully to itself.

Some of the most basic and most puzzling features of the detailed working out of Heidegger's problem will be the theme of the series of studies contained in the main part (Part II) of this book. Formidable difficulties of thought and language will encounter us there, but they are, in the last resort, only the visible outcrop of far simpler, much more basic difficulties that arise from the nature of the problem itself. To consider these briefly is the immediate and final task of the present exposition of Heidegger's question.

The first difficulty is not peculiar to Heidegger, but characterizes all ontological inquiry. It is a curious feature of *Sein und Zeit* that while it evidently addresses itself first and foremost to the philosophical world, Heidegger by no means takes a genuine understanding of ontology for granted. On the contrary, he constantly stresses the unique character of ontology: that its proper theme is being; that being is nothing like beings or their real properties and qualities and cannot be derived from our experience of them; and, above all, that to realize all this is the first indispensable step toward any philosophical understanding whatever.

Heidegger's frequent recurrence to this theme is so marked that one would be inclined to ascribe it to some special circumstances connected with *Sein und Zeit,* were it not that the same tendency becomes even more pronounced in Heidegger's later works. In these, the reader is constantly invited not to accept on hearsay, or be content with a merely verbal comprehension of the statement that being only "is" in the understanding and not in things, but to take his first step into philosophy genuinely by experiencing for himself the impossibility of finding the *is* in any of the things which are concretely accessible to him. (Cf., e.g. Denken, p. 107.)

Why is this step into philosophy so difficult to take? Partly because being is much less easy to grasp than beings, but partly also because experiencing things in terms of their being seems so natural to us as if it could not be otherwise. The tree, for instance, presents itself to the merest idle glance as something that *is;* it seems to bring its *is* along with itself. The impression is hard to eliminate that the *is* somehow belongs to the tree just as much as its shape, its color, the texture of its bark, the glossiness of its leaves. A little thought, however, will show that all these things are something, they belong to the realm of beings, so that we already understand them in terms of the *are*. We may examine the tree further, we may even think of the things we cannot directly experience, such as the processes of life going on in the tree, growth, nutrition, chemical changes, etc. But again, all these things are something, they belong to beings, and not one of them can give us the slightest hint or clue how we have come by the *is* and the *are*. Only one thing is certain: being is not something in addition to beings, but is the way in which these beings come to our understanding. They themselves can therefore never explain how we have come to understand them the way we do.

If the *is* can be found anywhere, it can evidently be found only in ourselves. But when we turn to ourselves, what do we find? Sensations, thoughts, feelings, desires—and these also are something, although not in the same way as the tree. Strictly speaking, we should not talk of our thoughts and feelings as though they were objects, but should say: I am feeling so and so; I am thinking this or that; I am experiencing such and such a sensation, and so forth. It turns out, then, that the *am* is already understood in all that we can concretely grasp in ourselves, just as much as the *is* is understood in the tree. The *am*, far from being more easily cornered than the *is*, seems to be even more elusive. We never seem to be able, as it were, to get "behind" it, but, on the contrary, it is there before us in every concrete experience of ourselves.

Our constant familiarity with the *is* and the *am* brings about a difficulty which has a special bearing on Heidegger's problem, the difficulty of genuinely experiencing how strange and even uncanny it is that we should understand ourselves and other beings in terms of the *am* and the *is*. Without some such experience, Heidegger's thought can indeed be comprehended as an intellectual construction, but the philosophic passion and excitement which are almost palpable in *Sein und Zeit,* and which alone could sustain the stupendous effort of thought embodied in this work, remain strange and baffling.

The commonplace familiarity of our understanding of being not only makes it hard to appreciate what Heidegger is "worrying about," but even raises a doubt whether his undertaking is not doomed to failure. Is it not hopeless to try to find out how our understanding of being is possible, when it is so near us that we can never get away from it? There is, according to Heidegger, one possibility: although being is always manifest to us, we can experience it in a new way, when it suddenly loses its matter-of-course familiarity. It is dread that reveals the commonplace in its utter strangeness and uncanniness. Dread singles each man out and brings him elementally face to face with the *that I am.* Hence the incomparable revelatory power of this basic mood and its methodological importance to an inquiry which seeks to penetrate through man's being to the meaning of being as such.

But the *that I am,* as Heidegger insists, can only be understood by a man in his own unique, factual existence. The remarkable ontological "circle-structure" of man's being, to which Heidegger repeatedly draws attention, leads us to the inmost meaning of the problem of being. On the one hand, the manifestness of being a priori determines man's whole way to be, enabling him first of all to exist as man, but, on the other hand, being requires and needs the unique, factual existence of a man for its manifestness. The "circularity" of the problem of being, however, is totally different from the "vicious circle" which may lie in a deductive proof, nor must it be thought of as a geometrical circle: it is a circling, whereby being and man circle round each other. The circularity of its problem is not a secret weakness at the heart of philosophy, but is its distinction. The task is not to avoid or suppress the circle, but to find the right way to get into it. The way found by Heidegger in *Sein und Zeit* has been briefly indicated: the approach to being is made through the analysis of the being of man. If we now ask whether there are other ways of "getting into the circle," the question aims at taking *Sein und Zeit* out of the isolation in which we have hitherto discussed it, and showing its place in Heidegger's thought as a whole.

The extraordinary difference between the two divisions we have of *Sein und Zeit* and Heidegger's later works has been the subject of much comment. The change is indeed startling enough to have given rise to the opinion that there is a complete break between *Sein und Zeit* and other early works, and those that come after. The manifest untenability of this view, however, soon led to the opposite extreme. The tendency in recent years has been to minimize the difference and ascribe it mainly to a change of theme, of style and language. While this view is not unsound, it still fails to go to the heart of the matter. What changes in Heidegger's later works is his way of "getting into the circle": being is no longer approached through man's understanding, but rather it is man's understanding which is approached through the manifestness of being. Only some such change could explain why so fundamental a concept as the "horizon of understanding" completely disappears from Heidegger's later thought. (Cf. Ge, pp. 38 ff.) Through a lifetime of philosophical activity, embodied in a wide range of works, Heidegger asks the same question, but he illuminates it by different ways of circling the same circle.

PART TWO

Basic Features and Problems of Sein und Zeit

◆§ Introductory

The first question usually addressed to a work of such universal scope as Heidegger's is how its theme has been divided and articulated. This question is of special importance in approaching *Sein und Zeit,* because, unless it is properly answered at the start, the whole treatise remains incomprehensible. As a fundamental ontology, *Sein und Zeit* differs radically from other ontologies which divide the realm of beings into regions and subregions. What is articulated in *Sein und Zeit* is not the all of beings, but man's way to be, and that means at the same time his way to understand being. Its articulation gives the following threefold unity:

1. Man understands first and foremost himself in his own being. This being is called by Heidegger *existence* (*Existenz*). The full structure of man's being, whose difference from existence will be discussed presently, receives the name of *care* (*Sorge*).

2. Man understands himself as being in a *world.* An understanding of world is an essential, irreducible constituent

of man's way of existing. The inquiry into the being of world goes hand in hand with the analysis of man's existence. The ontological structure of world is called by Heidegger *the worldishness of world (die Weltlichkeit der Welt)*.*

3. An understanding of his own being in a world enables man to meet other beings within the world and disclose them in *their* being. Some of these beings are like himself; they are fellowmen, whose being has the same character of existence as his own. Some are unlike himself; they are things in the strict sense of the word, and their being has the character of *reality (Vorhandenheit, Realität)*. The inquiry into the being of other beings goes hand in hand with the analysis of man's own existence (self) and of world.

As this short sketch already indicates, Heidegger unfolds his theme, in its threefold articulation, as a single unity. It is true that he may specially turn his attention now to man's self, now to world, and so on, but since these are in advance seen as articulations of a single understanding of being, the highlighting of one does not plunge the other two into darkness but brings them simultaneously to greater clarity. Heidegger conducts his inquiry as the driver of a three-in-hand handles his team, flicking now one horse, now another, but urging them forward all the time as one single team.

Heidegger is well aware that his approach may lay him open to the charge of being purely "subjective." Hence it is his constant concern to correct such misapprehensions, by stress-

* The noun *Weltlichkeit* and the adjective *weltlich* would ordinarily be translated by "worldliness" and "worldly." These words, unfortunately, have so definite a meaning in English as to be quite unusable in the context of *Sein und Zeit*. The expressions "worldishness" and "worldish" have the advantage of prohibiting the substitution of a familiar meaning for Heidegger's, as well as permitting parallel constructions with two other key concepts, *räumlich* and *zeitlich*. Their normal meaning, "spatial" and "timely," would be misleading, and they will therefore be rendered as "spaceish" and "timeish." As we shall see in due course, man is worldish, spaceish, timeish, i.e. world-forming, space-disclosing, time-originating.

ing that man's understanding of his own being in a world is precisely what gives him access to other beings and gives them the chance to show themselves in what and how they are. What is important is that the approach to things should be appropriate to their way of being, so that they can show themselves genuinely as they are. The most difficult among all beings to approach, however, is man himself, owing to his tendency to cover over his understanding of his own being by giving himself away to things.

Finding proper access both to man and to other beings, and securing original evidence for every conclusion reached, is Heidegger's constant preoccupation throughout *Sein und Zeit;* and the method he employs is one founded and developed by Husserl. Heidegger's method, in fact, is an application and adaptation of Husserl's phenomenology to his own problems. But it should be pointed out straightaway that this method is one of the grave difficulties of *Sein und Zeit* for those readers who are unfamiliar with Husserl's work, even the basic principles of which are hard to grasp. And just because they are, a discussion of phenomenology has been deferred to the seventh chapter of this part, though the logical order would require it to be placed at the beginning.

One of the characteristics of *Sein und Zeit,* owing largely to its method, is the marked difference between Divisions One and Two, and there is no doubt that if Division Three were added to the work, it would prove different again from what has gone before. The peculiar "phasing" of the investigation poses a problem for anyone writing a general introduction to *Sein und Zeit.* At this stage, therefore, the present writer has deemed it best to set out Heidegger's principal themes in separate studies, only one of which, the eighth, belongs exclusively to Division Two. The series of studies contained in this part are grouped as follows:

I. *The being of man.* The unique character of man's being is discussed in contrast to the being (reality) of things. The meaning of existence and care is provisionally explained, and the conclusion reached that man's being must be characterized as a *finitely free being.* The basic ways in which man is "free" to exist are then examined. This is followed by an explanation of the most important technical terminology of *Sein und Zeit,* concluding with a separate discussion of the meaning of *Dasein* and of its possible renderings in English.

II. *The worldishness of world.* The fundamental structure of man's being as being-in-the-world is the subject. Because of its exceptional difficulty, Heidegger's idea of world is here treated at considerable length. Then follows a discussion of theory and practice, and of the meaning of *Umwelt.*

III. *The reality of beings within the world.* The reality of the beings man meets within his world will prove to be understandable in two main ways: as substantial reality and as handy reality (*Vorhandenheit* and *Zuhandenheit*). These are distinguished and explained.

IV. *Being-with others and being-oneself.* The self in relation to other selves, and the repercussions on one's own self of being together with others in the world, are the themes unfolded in this chapter. The inquiry leads to the exposition of the fundamentally "falling" (disowned) way in which man is mostly himself in his everyday existence.

V. *The basic mood of dread and the being of man as care.* The culmination of Division One in the analysis of dread and in the exposition of the structure of care is presented in a summarized form and elucidated as far as possible.

VI. *Truth, being and existence.* Heidegger's existential interpretation of truth, and the way in which existence and being essentially belong together with the phenomenon of truth, are the subjects of this study.

VII. *The concept of phenomenology.* Heidegger's explanation of the concept of phenomenology is summarized and the importance of the phenomenological method for *Sein und Zeit* discussed. A few steps into Husserl's phenomenology are taken, and the point at which Heidegger diverges from Husserl is indicated.

VIII. *A preview of the tasks and problems of Division Two.* A short outline is given of the theme and development of Division Two, serving the twofold purpose of a preliminary introduction to more detailed study, and of indicating the perspective in which Division One must be seen to be fully understood.

IX. *Conclusion.* The question is raised here whether the solution to Heidegger's problem can be discerned from the two divisions of *Sein und Zeit* and from other works succeeding it. The conclusion is reached that, although not in full detail, the gist of Heidegger's answer is clear beyond doubt, and an attempt is made to indicate the essentials of the answer Heidegger gives to his own question.

☙ I The Being of Man

1.

a) EXISTENCE AND CARE, IN CONTRAST TO REALITY

"Man exists."

This frequently repeated sentence is the hardest to understand in the whole of *Sein und Zeit*. Its difficulty has to be specially stressed at this point, not only because the sentence itself looks simple, but because it might be thought that it should be understandable already on the basis of our preceding discussions. In fact, we are still only slightly prepared for it. There is only one thing which is already certain: the sentence cannot be a statement of fact. Different as a fundamental ontology may be from other ontologies, it must share with them the general character of ontological statements. Their distinction is that they do not tell us about facts, but about the way in which something must a priori, necessarily, be by virtue of its own essence. Heidegger's sentence must conform to a general type, which may be formulated as follows: Insofar as there is an X at all (e.g. a material thing, nature, space, number, language, etc.), it must a priori, by essential necessity, be in such and such a way, otherwise it could not be X. Accordingly, "man exists" tells us: Insofar as there is a man at all, he must by essential necessity be in the way of "existence," otherwise he could not be a man.

The character of Heidegger's sentence makes it clear that, in its context, the term *exist* cannot have the usual meaning of *real existence*. If it had, Heidegger would be saying nothing about the distinctively human way of being, but would be giving us a pure tautology. Granted, however, that Heidegger is really saying something essential about man, the term *exist* can only mean the unique way in which man is: he *is* so that he understands himself in his being. To be in this way, i.e. to exist, is according to Heidegger the "essence" of man.

The expressions *to exist* and *existence* are in *Sein und Zeit* exclusively reserved for man.* The "real existence" of beings other than man is called by Heidegger "real being" *(Vorhandensein)*, and the structure of this mode of being is called "reality" *(Realität)*. The living-being of plants and animals is only occasionally differentiated from the real-being of things, although Heidegger often stresses the difference between them and urges the need for an ontology of life. This task, however, cannot be taken in hand in *Sein und Zeit*, because it requires for its basis an already completed fundamental analysis of man: the full structure of man's being would have to be reduced and deprived of its uniquely "existential" features to arrive at what must necessarily be in order that merely-living-being should be possible. (Cf. e.g. SZ, p. 50.)

The basic distinction drawn in *Sein und Zeit* is thus be-

* Since the words "exist" and "existence" are indispensable in English, they will occasionally be used in this book for beings other than man. They will then stand in quotation marks and have the meaning of real existence. "Existent" and "nonexistent" will be used in a similar way.

tween the existence of man and the reality of beings that are not man. "To exist" and "to be real" are the two main ways in which beings can be. A real thing like a stone *is* so that it is essentially hidden to itself in its being. Its reality is characterized by a certain passivity, in the sense that it is manifest only to us, but not to the stone itself. Hence the stone is necessarily indifferent to its own being, or, more precisely, it is in such a way that it is incapable even of indifference.

At the other end of the scale, man exists in an actively disclosing way. The disclosure concerns first and foremost man himself: it is his own being that man most originally understands. This understanding, moreover, does not belong to man in general, but belongs to each man singly and uniquely. It is only in his own factual existence that a man can understand: "I myself am this man; this being is *mine.*" The extreme individuation of man, that to each one his being is manifest as *my* being, is an essential and therefore "universal" character of existence. Man is thrown into and delivered over to the being which is his and which he *has* to be: his ability to be this being is for him at stake *(es geht um)*.

In the three words, *es geht um,* Heidegger gives us a first hint of the peculiarly "out-going" and "fore-going" structure of existence, but, as often happens, the hint is unavoidably lost in translation. The general meaning of *es geht um,* "it is at stake," or, to quote the rendering given in *Being and Time,* "it is the issue," is certainly intended by Heidegger: for man, it is his own being that is at stake. But it is a distinction of Heidegger's language that many of his key words and phrases directly exhibit the thought to be conveyed and carry the attention forward to other important ideas with which they are closely connected. In the phrase we are considering, for instance, the key word *um,* "for," in advance refers us to the basic character of existence as the original and primary *Umwillen,* "for the sake of." Since for man his own being is at stake, his existence has the basic character of *for the sake of*. The connection, which Heidegger shows simply and directly by the language itself, can only be established in translation by long and roundabout explanations. On the other hand, such explanations can often be very helpful in introducing a new theme and leading into the detailed analyses in which Heidegger painstakingly works out his theme and brings the requisite evidence. Needless to say, without a thorough study of the latter even the most correct comprehension of Heidegger's key concepts hangs rootlessly in the air.

Our present discussion can conveniently take its start from the *for the sake of* as the fundamental character of existence. What does *for the sake of* imply? It undoubtedly suggests something like a purpose, an aim, an end, and not merely a partial end, which may in turn be used as means to some further end, but what is usually called an "end in itself." Heidegger, however, does not have a specific end in view, which may be either chosen by us or given to us, but seeks to explain, among other things, how man must a priori be in order to be capable of conceiving something like an end or aim at all. To understand this more concretely, let us start from the familiar experience of pursuing some definite aim and consider what is necessarily required to make this experience possible.

The most obvious characteristic of an aim is that it cannot be a fact, something that a man already is or has: according to common experience, an aim is something that a man has "before him," "ahead of him." When a man sets himself a specific aim, for instance, of climbing Mount Everest, he conceives it as a possibility which he may or may not achieve sometime in the future. Until then, he lets this possibility in advance determine all the steps he takes here and now: he undergoes most rigorous training, exposes himself to hardship and danger, bends his energies toward organizing his expedition, collecting the equipment, etc.—and all this for the sake of a possibility which may never be realized, and on whose outcome he stakes his life.

Remarkable as the pursuit and achievement of such an aim is, for Heidegger it is even more remarkable how man must be to be capable of conceiving something like an aim at all. For this, he must be able to throw himself forward into a future, to discover as yet completely "nonexistent" things and events and take his direction from them for what should be done "here and now." Above all, he must be able to understand himself not only in that *I am,* but in the possibility that *I can be* (e.g. I can be the Mount Everest climber), and thus come toward himself, so to speak, clad in his possibilities. In other words, man must be able to transcend, to go out beyond himself as he already is to the *possibilities* of his being, and it is this unique way of being which Heidegger calls existing.

If man were merely real in every here and now, and his existence were made up from a series of hops from now to now, he would be incapable of disclosing possibilities, of understanding himself in his own ability-to-be *(Seinkönnen),* and so of conceiving any aim or end at all. But more than that: the remarkable way in which man exists in and from his possibilities is not merely incidentally tacked onto his *I am,* but is the way in which man most essentially is and understands himself. To be constantly ahead of, in advance of, itself is the basic character of existence, and is made possible by the "fore-throw" structure of understanding, which will be more fully discussed in the next chapter. The *I am* is primarily understood from the fore-throw of an *I can be* (I am able to be); man exists primarily from the future.

In the phrases, "it is at stake," and "for the sake of," Heidegger gives us a first hint of how man is disclosed to himself in his possible-being (I can be), and so brings us to the heart of the concept of existence, because it is in the disclosure of possibilities that the utmost illumination of man's own self is gathered. To exist as himself, moreover, is not merely one of man's possibilities among many others; it is his *ownmost possibility.* What Heidegger means by "ownmost possibility" *(eigenste Möglichkeit)* is, of course, still obscure, and it is in the nature of such concepts that they can never be wrenched open all at once or be fully penetrated in any single approach. All that is clear at the moment is that the difficulty and problem of existence gathers itself in the concept of possibility, and to clarify this must be our immediate aim.

As soon as we begin to consider what is meant by possibility, we are dismayed by the diffuseness and elusiveness of this concept. The diffuseness shows itself in the many different ways and senses in which the concept can be legitimately applied. First and most frequently, we talk of possibilities in an empirical sense, meaning that this or that can happen to a thing, or that such and such occurrences may or may not take place. These possibilities are contingencies which are applicable, in Heidegger's sense, only to real beings (things). It is true that this and that can also happen to man, but, just because for him his own being is at stake, even the accidents that can befall him have quite a different meaning from the contingencies that can happen to a thing. Further, we talk of possibilities in the sense of potentialities, e.g. the potentiality of a seed to grow into a tree, or the possibilities of a man to develop his inborn faculties and dispositions.

These factual possibilities, however, are obviously not what Heidegger has primarily in view in his inquiry. Let us turn, therefore, to the philosophical meaning of possibility. Here again we find that the term has a wide range. First, there is the empty, logical concept of possibility as the sheer thinkability of something, i.e. something can be thought without contradiction or absurdity. Further, possibility is one of the modalities or modal categories of being, in contrast to actuality and necessity. Here possibility means what is *only* possible, but need not be actual and is never necessary. Traditionally, possibility is held to be "lower" than actuality and necessity, whereas Heidegger emphasizes that, as the ontological character of existence, possible-being is "higher" than any actuality. (Cf. SZ, pp. 143 f.) Further, the essence, the whatness of a thing is traditionally also called possibility: the essence is that which makes it possible for a thing to be as it is.

Possibility in the last-named sense is relevant also to Heidegger, who calls it *Ermöglichung*: it is the constitutive "power" which "empowers," which "enables," "makes capable of . . ." When Heidegger speaks of the "essence" *(Wesen)* of man, he usually means possibility in the sense just defined. Accordingly, the well-known sentence that "the 'essence' of man lies in his existence" (cf. SZ, p. 42) does not mean, as some interpretations would have it, that man first of all "really exists" (really occurs) and then proceeds to produce his own essence, i.e. to make himself into who he is by exercising his freedom of choice, but means: Understanding himself in his own ability-to-be enables man to be man in the most essential respect, namely in respect of his self.

Confusing as the many meanings of possibility already are, an even greater difficulty arises from the elusiveness of this concept. There is something quite ungraspable about a possibility, even when we think of it in the most concrete sense as the possibility of some real happening. The question is whether this ungraspability is due to some failure in our thinking, or whether it lies in the very being of possibility itself. In what way can a possibility *be* at all?

To answer this question, let us consider an empirical possibility in contrast to an empirical fact. Supposing on a journey we approach a certain district and come on a scene of devastation caused by an earthquake the day before, the disaster comes to our understanding as a fact which, having occurred, *is* and cannot be altered or undone. Now let us suppose that we approach another district and find people fleeing from it, because an earthquake had been predicted for the following day. This earthquake obviously comes to our understanding in quite a different way from the one we experienced as a fact. What and how *is* this earthquake which is not yet, but is coming? It is not a fact; it is not real; it does not "exist" at all; and yet it *is*—as a possibility. The whole being of this earthquake lies in our understanding it as a possibility, as something that can be. The disaster that has already happened is a real event, regardless of whether any man discovers it and understands it in its reality. But an earthquake that has not yet happened, *only* is insofar as there is man to discover it in its possible-being. Had the earthquake tomorrow not been predicted, and it really happened, it would always be discoverable *as* a fact, but never again as it is now, *as* a possibility which bears down on us in its uncertainty and threat, not the less threatening because it may not really happen, after all.

Events which come toward us from the future evidently only *are* as possibilities, as events that *can be*. The remarkable thing about them is that their being is in advance determined by a *not*. The *can be* in itself implies that it can also *not* be. It would be impossible for us to understand the "can" unless we understood it as "possibly not." Even when we are so certain of something that we say it *must* be, we are implying that it *cannot* be otherwise, because the conditions are such that all possibilities except one are *impossible*. It does not matter, therefore, how some future event is disclosed, e.g. whether the earthquake is predicted by the strictest scientific calculation, or on empirical evidence, or by casting a horoscope. This determines only the ground and degree of its certainty, or likelihood, but does not in the least take away the *not* which in advance belongs to our understanding of possibilities as such.

It is clear, therefore, that the disquieting elusiveness of possibilities lies in their very being, and does not primarily arise from the imperfection of our thinking or the uncertainty of our knowledge. But if already an empirical possibility, such as we have discussed, is hard to grasp, how much more so Heidegger's interpretation of existence as "possible-being," (ability-to-be). The manifold implications of this concept are for the most part still obscure, but one meaning at least is beginning to emerge: existence is that way of being which is capable of going out beyond what is to what is not, and so disclose not actual things or beings, but the *possibility* of beings, the being of beings in the mode of possibility.

But how is such a remarkable thing possible that man can understand the being of something that is not? Presumably only so that the *not* in advance reveals itself in and with his own being. The key phrase, *es geht um,* it is at stake, gives us a first hint of how the *not* is originally manifest to man. How could his own being be at stake for him, unless it were in advance disclosed as a being he stands to lose? Man exists, i.e. understands himself in his being from the constant possibility that he can also *not* be. This harsh and forbidding *not* is far from being a mere negativity, an "empty nothing." It is in the highest sense positive: it enables man to understand the possibilities of his own being and those of other beings: it is the source of possibility as such.

Understanding himself in the jeopardy of his being reveals to man that the being he stands to lose is solely and singly his, and not another's. The *not* that can end his being threatens him alone in his own ability to be, and so brings him into the uniqueness of a finite self. To exist as himself is man's *ownmost* possibility: it is most his own as against his other possibilities of being with other beings. His ability to be himself is disclosed from the utmost end of a man's being, and cannot therefore be referred to any further "end." The possibility of his own end, moreover, does not reveal itself to a man as some indifferent "fact," but strikes at him in the heart of his being. Hence a man's ability to be can never be the means to some end beyond itself, but is for its own sake.

Accordingly, when Heidegger says that man exists for the sake of himself, he is not advocating, as might easily be thought, a ruthless selfishness, but is stating the ontological problem of who is and how there can be a finite self. If in his concrete existence man is able to understand something like a "for your sake," "for his sake," "for this and that" at all, and so set himself specific aims and ends, it is only because his own self is in advance disclosed to him in its finite possibilities as the primary and original "for the sake of." (Cf. Grund, p. 37.)

Man's existence is thus at the opposite extreme from the reality of a thing, which is so that it can neither care nor not care for its own being. Man not only cares, but, as Heidegger's interpretation will show, man's being *is* care.

The concept of care, which is elucidated only at the end of Division One (chap. 6), is apt to lead to confusion and bewilderment. Why, the reader may not unreasonably ask, does Heidegger first define man's being as existence, only to show in the end that it really is care? To make matters even more difficult, the elaborate care-structure worked out by Heidegger at the end of Division One refuses to show the slightest resemblance to any care we may have concretely experienced: it is, as Heidegger himself stresses, a purely ontological-temporal concept, whose meaning *(Sinn)* will be shown in Division Two to be time.

The reason why the concept of care cannot be elucidated earlier in the inquiry lies in the extraordinary complexity of man's being, which can be brought to light only gradually in the course of a long and difficult analysis. Heidegger, it is true, announces already at the beginning (SZ, p. 57) that the being of man is to be interpreted as care. The trouble is that this preliminary announcement, as well as all further references to care in the course of Division One, remain basically incomprehensible without a much fuller explanation than Heidegger stops to give. To alleviate the reader's difficulties, we shall now attempt a provisional sketch of what is meant by care, and especially of the relation in which it stands to existence.

Care is Heidegger's name for how the whole man is, and how he wholly is. But man is in an extremely complex way, which can be articulated into three main structures: existence (self), thrownness (facticity) and fallenness. The first of these three articulations of care we have already discussed: in existing, man is constantly out beyond himself, throwing himself forward into what is not, disclosing it as a possibility. This original disclosure is not a conscious discovery or a thinking out of what might come, but lies in the fore-throw structure of care, which Heidegger calls *understanding*. The temporal meaning of this "forwardness" of care is evidently the future. In Heidegger's interpretation, the future will turn out to be the primary mode or ecstasis (standing-out-of-itself) of time.

But man can only be ahead of, beyond himself, insofar as he already is. Bringing his possibilities toward himself, he necessarily comes back to himself as he already, in fact, is. The "fact" of his being, which Heidegger calls facticity, is revealed to man as his being already here, thrown into a world, left to himself to be as he can in the midst of beings, upon which he is dependent. The whence and whither of his being are hidden, but the fact "that I am and have to be" stares him in the face in inexorable mysteriousness. (Cf. SZ, p. 136.) The curious phenomenal character of the *I am* is that it can never be grasped except as *I already am,* i.e. *I am as having been.* The time-character of man's thrownness is the past, the has-been.

Fallenness, or as it might be more fully paraphrased, "falling captive to the world" *(Verfallen),* is a trend toward the world which is basic to man's being, and which has already been mentioned as man's tendency to give himself away to things, to scatter himself in his occupations in company with other people, literally to disown himself. The ecstatic character of fallenness is the present.

A genuine understanding of this short sketch is not possible at this stage: its purpose is to show how the three main structures of man's being—existence (self), thrownness (facticity) and fallenness—are articulations of the original whole of care, and not parts or components of which the whole is made up. And care itself, it should be observed, is the unity of time—future, past and present. Even so, this might be misleading were Heidegger's interpretation of time not kept in view, an interpretation designed to show that man does not merely exist "in time" like a thing, but "originates," or "brings himself to ripeness" as time *(sich zeitigt).* Man himself exists as time—when there is no man, there is no time.

But now to return to the question of existence: just because it is as care that man exists in such a complex and excentric way—ahead of himself, thrown back onto himself, losing himself—we can legitimately say that "Man exists," meaning the whole of his being and not merely a part of it. In the articulated whole of care, it is true, existence names only one structure, but it is a structure in a whole which is so originally one that any one of its articulations necessarily implies the others. When we say "Man exists," we are already saying, though not explicitly expressing it, that he exists factually (facticity, thrownness), and that thus factually existing, he is already falling away from himself to the things he meets within his world. Similarly, when we speak of thrownness, we already imply that this thrown man *is* in the way of existence, because only in coming back to himself in the possibilities of his being can man *find himself* already thrown into a world, and not merely occur in it like a thing. Similarly, when we speak of fallenness, we are already implying existence and thrownness, for only a man who understands his being in a world *can* lose himself to the things he meets within it. For a stone, it is impossible to lose itself.

Nevertheless, it is not without reason that Heidegger says emphatically "Man exists," rather than "Man is thrown," or "Man is falling away from himself." In the articulated whole of care, existence has a certain precedence, it plays a "leading" role: in it is gathered the most unique character of man's being and the possibility of its utmost illumination. As the "fore-going" way of care, existence may be called in a preeminent sense the "light" of man's being. At the same time, as Heidegger always emphasizes, man has an "ontological circle-structure": the "light" of existence is only possible to a thrown and fallen being. The same thought is implied in one of the formal announcements *(formale Anzeige)* which Heidegger gives of existence: "Each man *is* his possibility, and does not merely 'have' it by way of a property, like a thing." (Cf. SZ, p. 42.)

How is this cryptic sentence to be understood? A thing, according to Heidegger, cannot *be* its possibility, but may in an imprecise way be said to "have" it. We say, for instance, that a meteorite "has" the possibility of falling in space, of entering the earth's atmosphere, becoming overheated, exploding, etc. As we have seen earlier, the whole being of a possibility lies in its being disclosed *as* a possibility. From where are the possibilities of the meteorite disclosable at all? From its essence, its whatness, i.e. its being a material thing. The possibility of its motion, heat, divisibility, etc. is manifest from the properties of matter and not from its own unique being. The meteorite is only a sample of the possibilities of material things in general, which do not in the least require the "existence" of this particular meteorite for their disclosure.

With man, on the contrary, the factual existence of a unique self is required to be its own possibility. The essence of man is to understand his being as the possibility that is singly and uniquely his own. This possibility cannot be disclosed by some "man in general," but only by a single man, to whom it is his own being that is at stake. Each man, therefore, *is* his possibility—only his own factual existence can manifest itself as the possibility that is uniquely his. The circle-structure of man's being comes to evidence, and must do so, whenever he is regarded in the light of his own essence —and his essence is centered in that "forward-going" way of care which Heidegger calls existence.

It is clear, therefore, that if man is to be explained fundamentally, from the way of being distinctive of him, and not merely empirically, from some specific point of view, for instance, for medical or sociological purposes, within the strict limits which such purposes prescribe, the inquiry must in advance have the whole man in view in his own unique existence. It cannot reduce man to something less than he is in himself, and explain him from *what* he is, from his genus and species, his environment and his society. On the contrary, the inquiry will have to show, among other things, what are the ontological conditions of the possibility that man *can* be social, and why it is that a world not only essentially belongs to him, but that he tends to lose himself to it.

But, it may be asked, is it not strange that Heidegger should consider man's tendency to lose himself so fundamental to him, when at the same time he holds that to exist as himself is the very essence of man? This strange inconsistency, however, will prove to be only apparent when we turn to a topic which has not yet been touched upon, namely the various possibilities which lie in existence itself. In developing this theme, we shall also come to understand more fully the sentence discussed above: "Each man *is* his possibility . . ." The theme to be considered now may be briefly summed up in the following thesis: Existence is in itself a *free* way of being.

How is *freedom* to be understood in an ontological sense? It obviously cannot be what we usually mean by freedom, e.g. the ability to choose this course of action rather than that, or to pursue this end in preference to another one. All these "freedoms," all acts of will which aim at achieving this end rather than that, already presuppose that we understand the possible being of what is aimed at and that we can direct ourselves to it as a "for its sake." For Heidegger, freedom means the original disclosure of being, and in a preeminent sense our understanding of our own being as the primary *for the sake of* (*Umwillen;* literally, for the will of). This freedom is the original "will" which brings before itself its own possibilities as "for the will of." The disclosure of the possibilities of his being sets man free for different *ways* of being himself. It is, therefore, not a priori determined by the structure of existence *how* a man's being is to be his. On the contrary, it enables man to relate himself to his own ability-to-be in profoundly different ways, and so leaves it open how each factual existence is a self. Existence is thus a *free* way of being, because the possibility of various modifications lies in its own structure.

But, as we have seen, all possibility, all *can be,* is in advance determined by a *not.* In transcending to his possibilities, man *is* free, but always and only in the way in which he can be free, namely finitely. It lies in the nature of finite freedom that, in giving possibilities, it at the same time withdraws them. Each man *is* his possibility, but always and only in one of the ways which are open to him. A man cannot exist in a vague generality, but only in one or another of his definite possibilities. Each man is one of his possibilities, the others he is *not.* It now begins to be faintly visible why notness and nothing enter so importantly into Heidegger's idea of being. This *not,* which reveals itself so inexorably to each man, makes possible and articulates through and through his existence as a *finitely free being.*

For a proper approach to *Sein und Zeit,* nothing could be more helpful than to grasp, however roughly and provisionally, the idea of a finitely free being. It is this idea which in advance guides and articulates Heidegger's whole inquiry, and determines the way in which he gets to grips with his subject. The essence of man cannot be defined by *what* he is, by the attributes and qualities of a rational animal, because man is finitely free: his fundamental possibilities do not lie somewhere outside himself, but in his own being as care, which is "free" to modify itself in certain basic ways. The essence of this being lies in existence (self). *How* man is can therefore only be defined by the basic modes or manners *(Seinsart)* in which it is possible for him to exist, i.e. to be a self. It is from man's basic possibilities that the inquiry must take its lead. Hence each division of *Sein und Zeit* is an analysis of man's being in a different mode of existence. What the basic possibilities of existence are will be the task of the next section to consider.

b) THE TWO BASIC WAYS OF EXISTING: OWNED AND DISOWNED EXISTENCE. THE UNDIFFERENTIATED MODALITY OF EVERYDAYNESS

Heidegger calls the two basic possibilities of existence *Eigentlichkeit* and *Uneigentlichkeit*, the usual translation of these terms being "authenticity" and "inauthenticity." This translation, while it is perfectly correct, shifts the weight of the words from the center to the circumference. Their weight, as Heidegger explicitly says, lies in *eigen*, which simply means *own*. We shall therefore speak of owned and disowned existence, or, what means the same thing, of being one's own self or a disowned self. Since, however, *owned* and *disowned* are very clumsy to use adverbially, we shall occasionally resort to such phrases as "to be a self properly" or "not-properly," where "properly" must be understood in the strictly literal sense of *proprius*, one's own.

The terminology adopted here, especially the word *disowned*, could easily be misleading if it were understood in the sense of an attitude deliberately taken up or a course of action willfully pursued by man toward himself. This would imply an interpretation of the self which is completely alien to Heidegger. What does Heidegger mean when he speaks of the self? Does he mean that man first of all exists, and then in addition he is or acquires something called a self? No. Heidegger means that man *is* a self in existing, i.e. in understanding that "I *myself* am this man; this being is *mine*." *How* a man is himself is determined by the way in which he lets his being be his. No man has freely chosen his being; he may not have wished it if he had had any say in the matter; nonetheless, he *can* freely take over his being as his own responsibility, he can turn to it face to face, letting it fully disclose itself as singly and uniquely his. Existing in this way, man is wholly his own self, according to the fullest possibility of his finite being. Or he can turn away from himself, not letting his being fully disclose itself as his own, covering over its finiteness by throwing himself into those "endless" possibilities that come to him from his world. Existing in this way, man disowns the possibility of the utmost illumination of which his being is capable and falls into the disguise which characterizes his lostness to the world.

While these basic ways of existing are neither subconscious "mechanisms" nor conscious and deliberate "attitudes," they definitely imply something like a "relation" of man to himself. Heidegger, in fact, frequently and explicitly speaks of the ways in which man can "relate himself" *(sich verhalten)* to himself, and means: man bears himself toward, holds himself in, stands fast in, the possibilities of his being in *one way or another,* not primarily by thinking about them, but by throwing himself into them as best he can. This "relation" is very near to what we have in mind when we speak of the way in which a man lives. It is in his "way of living" that a man stabilizes himself as the factual self he is, that he stands fast in the being he bears in his thrownness as care.

But if each man's being, regardless of *how* it is his, is yet essentially his own, it might be reasonable to suppose that he would tend to "own" his being, while a disowned existence would seem to be an exceptional falling away from the average, the norm. Heidegger's thesis, however, is that the opposite is the truth: man's fundamental tendency is to turn away from himself to a self-forgetful absorption in his occupations in company with other people. Before his existence can be properly his own, a man has usually to wrest it back from its lostness to the world.

In the first place and for the most part *(zunächst und*

zumeist), man understands himself not from his own being, but from what other people think. Instead of the utmost illumination of which he is capable, man exists in a sort of "public disclosedness," whose very publicity is a way of covering over that each man's being is singly his own. In the first place and for the most part, this is the way in which man is himself from day to day, his average day, his every day. Everydayness *(Alltäglichkeit)* is Heidegger's name for the average, undifferentiated way in which man exists over most of his lifetime, living unto the day, taking for variety what the day brings, what chances and events, what successes and failures come to him from his world. In his everydayness, man is so decisively orientated toward the world that the possibility of understanding himself from his own being remains obscured. When Heidegger speaks of an "indifferent" everydayness, he does not mean that this mode of existence ceases to be care, or that man no longer exists for the sake of himself, let alone that he exists neither in one definite way nor in another, but means that the difference between an owned and disowned self does not come to light, it remains undifferentiated.

For Heidegger's "Preparatory Fundamental Analysis of the Being of Man," it is precisely this undifferentiated everydayness which is of utmost importance, because it constitutes the *average* manner of man's being. But even in this leveled-down uniformity, man still exists, he still understands himself in his being. Man can only be average in the way of existence and not as an egg or an income is said to be average. Even in the extremity of disownment, man can never become merely real like a thing, or like an only-living-organism. His way of existing can be modified but can never become a different order of being.

The everyday mode of existence, just because it is nearest

and most familiar to us, has been consistently overlooked in philosophy, and its ontological importance has not been realized. As Heidegger's inquiry will show, traditional ontology draws its idea of reality not from the way it is originally manifest in man's everydayness, but from a secondary and derivative modification of it. A remarkable feature of Heidegger's analysis of everyday existence is to show the complex and mysterious character of this most familiar way of man's being. It remains the leading theme throughout Division One, while the owned way of existing becomes the main theme at the beginning of Division Two, preparing the way for the interpretation of the fundamental "timeishness" *(Zeitlichkeit)* of man's being.

c) THE ONTOLOGICAL-EXISTENTIAL TERMINOLOGY OF *Sein und Zeit*

Apart from Heidegger's special key words, such as "care," "thrownness," "worldishness," etc., there is the purely technical terminology of *Sein und Zeit* to be considered. The new theme of this work requires new terms, some of which are parallel to those of traditional ontology, and some are taken over from Husserl's phenomenology, often with a shift of meaning or emphasis. Among the latter, we have already come across "meaning" *(Sinn)* and "ontological structure" *(Seinsstruktur)*. We shall now consider the following terms:

(1) *Ontological—existential* (Ontologisch—existenzial)

These two terms are parallel. Understood in the strict sense, ontology should mean in *Sein und Zeit* only those inquiries that have for their theme the being of beings other than man. This restricted meaning of ontology, however, is not consistently adhered to by Heidegger, who often refers to his own analyses as "ontological," when they should be called "existential." The latter term applies only to man's being and to the inquiry which has man's being for its theme. This inquiry calls itself "existential," because it takes its lead from the essence of man, which lies in his existence. Its detailed analyses will show that each of the main structures of care, namely existence, facticity and fallenness, can be further analyzed into essential constituents *(konstitutive Momente)*. These are details in the whole which cannot be detached from the whole, but can be discerned and defined within it as essential to it and helping to make the whole as it is. All the a priori constituents and characters of man's being are given the general name of "existentials" by Heidegger. These require further discussion.

(2) *Categories—existentials* (Kategorien—Existenzialien)

These two terms are parallel. Categories are those most general characters of being that can be a priori predicated of things, e.g. things are of such and such *quality, quantity,* so and so *related,* etc. Categories are hence often called "ontological predicates." This is the general philosophical meaning of category, although the term has been variously interpreted in the course of history, and the "tables of categories" set up by different thinkers have varied accordingly. It may be remembered, for instance, that Aristotle includes time and place in his ten categories, whereas in Kant's transcendental philosophy time and space are taken out of the class of categories altogether and receive a new meaning as the a priori forms of intuition. For Heidegger, the decisive distinction is that categories are the a priori characters of the being of things, whereas existentials are the a priori characters of the being of man. These two, categories and existentials, are called by Heidegger the two main *characters of being (Seinscharaktere)*.

The new terminology introduced by Heidegger, however, is not merely a convenient way of making fine distinctions, but is demanded by the nature of Heidegger's theme. This can be especially well demonstrated by the difference between a category and an existential. A close study of *Sein und Zeit* shows that the existential characters of man have an "active" form, and the categorial characters of things a "passive" form. This is not an accident but expresses the difference between man and things: man in an active and transitive sense "constitutes" ("forms") being, while the being of things is necessarily a "constituted" being. Let us, for example, consider space. Man is "spaceish," i.e. he in an active way discloses space. The existential constituents of man's spaceishness are called by Heidegger "un-distancing" *(ent-fernen, Ent-fernung)*, i.e. bringing near, removing or diminishing distance; and "directing" *(ausrichten)*, i.e. directing himself or something else toward . . ., taking a direction to or from . . . Undistancing and directing are existentials, which show themselves as the categories of distantness (nearness) and directedness (e.g. to the left, above, below, etc.) in the spatial characters of a thing.

It is, however, not only spatially, but also in many other ways that man can relate himself or refer himself to things. The existential character of self-relating or self-referring *(Verweisung)* appears as the category of relatedness or referredness, which defines the being of things.

Only when the difference between an existential and a category has been grasped, does it become understandable what Heidegger means by saying that the characters of man's being are not "properties" but *ways* in which it is possible for him to be.* (Cf. SZ, p. 42.) All existentials, e.g. undistancing, directing, self-referring, etc., are *ways* in which man is, whereas

* This implies that all existentials answer the question: *how?* It is evident that the *how* must have a very much wider application in Heidegger's thought than it had traditionally. We cannot appropriately ask: "What is man?" and even the question: "Who is man?" applies to him only as a factual self. The primary and leading question concerning man's being is: "*How* is man?"

the corresponding categories show themselves as properties and attributes, i.e. the spatial properties, the attribute of relatedness, etc. whereby the being of things can be determined.

(3) *Fundamental ontological/existential constitution* (Ontologische/existenziale Grundverfassung or Seinsverfassung)

The basic meaning of "constitution" *(Konstitution)* was indicated in the preceding section. The active and transitive verb *to constitute, to make up, to form,* must be primarily heard in the noun *constitution.* In Husserl's phenomenology, the term refers to those activities of transcendental consciousness which constitute the essence, the whatness of beings in their familiar types. In other words, these activities originally form the categorial structure of the great ontological regions, which are divided by Husserl into nature and spirit, and subdivided into subregions such as material nature, animality, personal world, intersubjectivity, etc.

The original meaning of *constitution* necessarily implies a second meaning, namely an organized categorial whole which defines the essence of a region of beings, and it is in this sense that Heidegger uses the term *Seinsverfassung.* When the term is applied to man's being, Heidegger usually speaks of *existenziale Verfassung,* existential constitution. A similar meaning can be assigned to the term *Grundverfassung,* basic or fundamental constitution, but it should be noted that a fundamental constitution need not necessarily be sufficient *fully* to define the being under consideration.

This point will prove to be of some importance for understanding the role which the fundamental constitution of man, "being-in-the-world," plays in *Sein und Zeit.* Since we are not yet in a position to discuss this difficult structure, and show how and where it is deficient, let us try to understand the point in question by considering a more familiar example.

If we think, for instance, of nature, it is immediately evident that space must belong to its fundamental constitution, since material phenomena cannot show themselves at all except as being "in space." Descartes, indeed, holds *extension* to be the fundamental ontological character of material nature. The question relevant to our discussion is this: does the spatial constitution of nature, fundamental as it is, sufficiently and fully define its being? Evidently not, since it alone cannot explain the essential "materiality" of nature. As Husserl, for instance, points out, the merely extended thing of Descartes could never be distinguished from a phantom, a ghost of a thing. (Cf. Ideen II, pp. 36–37, further p. 40.) Materiality (substantiality) could never show itself if a thing appeared solely in and by itself, unrelated to other things. Only in its external relations can its materiality be constituted: the thing must show itself as identifiably the same under changing conditions. Something like interrelation (causality), which in turn already implies time, must therefore belong to the categorial structure of material nature as such.

The categorial whole constitutive of the being of things characterizes their mode of being as *reality*. The whole of existentials into which the being of man can be articulated constitutes the *existentiality* of existence.

(4) *A priori, "earlier"*

Even in our simplest awareness of a thing there lies already the disclosure of something like time, space, relation, etc. What already lies there in every experience as the condition of its possibility is said to be a priori, "earlier." It is generally agreed that the business of philosophy, i.e. philosophy in the strict and not the popular sense, is to inquire into the a priori, but different thinkers have given varying interpretations of how this concept is to be understood. Heidegger understands it as "fore-going and going-hand-in-hand-with" experience (*vorgängig und mitgängig*). Roughly speaking, this means: what is already there in experience as the condition of its possibility does not lie somewhere apart from and in a time before experience. On the other hand, it cannot be derived from or learned by experience: it goes before experience, taking it by the hand and leading it. Fore-going to any experience is the existentiality of man's existence, on the ground of which he is able to understand his own being, and let other beings show themselves in their being.

(5) *Ontic—existentiell* (Ontisch—existenziell)

The adjective "ontic" is the counterpart to "ontological": it characterizes beings, not their being. Anything that in any way "exists," is ontic. The synonym for ontic is "existent," the word to be understood in the traditional sense of real existence, and not in Heidegger's special sense. Approximations to ontic are: real, concrete, empirical, given in experience. While these terms can be used for ontic in certain contexts, they do not have nearly so wide a meaning. Heidegger uses the word *ontic* constantly, applying it to man as well as to things.

Existentiell is only approximately parallel to ontic and has a much more restricted meaning, applying only to man. Heidegger uses the word *existentiell* primarily to characterize the understanding we each have of our concrete existence and of all that belongs to it. For this, a theoretical insight into the a priori existential structure of our existence is not in the least necessary. A man may have no explicit philosophical understanding of himself, or may interpret his own being as reality; this does not prevent him from having a genuine and profound existentiell understanding of himself. Conversely, a philosophical insight does not guarantee that a man is existentielly transparent to himself in his concrete existence.

Summary

It may be found helpful to summarize Heidegger's technical terminology in the following schematic contrast:

existentiell	is parallel to	ontic
existential (adj.)	"	ontological
existential (noun)	"	category
existential structure	"	categorial structure
existential constitution	"	ontological constitution
existentiality	"	reality

It should be noted that Heidegger usually couples the terms existential-ontological, and sometimes also existentiell-ontic. The addition of *ontological* and *ontic* does not alter the meaning of *existential* and *existentiell,* but serves to remind the reader that the inquiry is not one of the traditional style: it is an existential ontology, which is simply another name for fundamental ontology. It must also be stressed once more that Heidegger frequently applies the simple terms ontological and ontic to man. This practice will be followed in this book when the long compound expressions would be too clumsy to use.

2. *Why does Heidegger call man* Dasein? *A discussion of the meaning of* Dasein

The question to be considered first is why Heidegger rejects the word *man* (*Mensch*) and adopts the term *Dasein.* His reasons have already been touched upon in previous discussions, so that it is sufficient at this stage to recapitulate the relevant points:

a) *Man is never a "what."* The word *man,* considered from a logical-grammatical point of view, is a collective noun like house, table, tree, etc. Nouns of this type gather concrete individuals into a class, and the class indicates the whatness of its members. But man is never a what: his essence (self) lies in his existence. His existential constitution sets him free for different modes of being himself. How a man exists can therefore never be determined by any whatness, and the word *man* is inappropriate to the kind of being man is.

b) *The being in which each man understands himself is his own.* The class name *man*, more precisely defined, is the name of a species of living beings, on a par with horse, sheep, sparrow, etc. The concrete individuals that belong to a species are regarded as cases or samples representing their species. But a man can never be merely a case or a sample of the species *man*, because what makes it possible for him to exist as man is not his species, but his understanding of himself in his being. For this reason, also, the word *man* has to be rejected as inadequate.

The *positive reason* which has led Heidegger to choose the term *Dasein* can be briefly indicated as follows: The fundamental characters of man's being are not properties and qualities, but ways in which it is possible for him to be. *Dasein* expresses being, and nothing else. It is a translation into German of the word *existentia*, and its usual meaning is simply *real existence*. It need hardly be said that, as Heidegger's name for man, *Dasein* can no more keep its traditional meaning than the word *existence*. Unfortunately, there is no expressive way in which *Dasein* can be translated into English, as an explanation of its meaning and form will clearly show.

Purely linguistically considered, *Da-sein* is a compound of two words, whose second component, *sein*, means simply *to be* or *being*. This *to be*, since it expresses the being of man, must be understood as the infinitive of the *am*, and not of the *is* of a thing. The first component, the *Da*, indicates a place, a here and a there, and this is why in some translations *Dasein* is rendered by "being-here" and in others by "being-there." In fact, *Da* is neither here nor there, but somewhere between the two, for which we have no exact equivalent in English; it is a much more open word than either here or there, and does not have a definitely localized meaning.

Is there any way in which *Da* and *Dasein* can be at least approximately expressed in English? Perhaps the best approach to it can be made by taking the phrases "there is . . ." and "there are . . ." for a starting point. In these phrases, the "there" evidently does not mean a definite place in which something occurs, but the whole phrase means the "thereness" of something. If we take "there-being" (there to be) as the infinitive of "there is . . . ," we arrive at the traditional meaning of *Dasein*: real existence, the real "thereness" of something.

But as for man, his there-being cannot mean merely the real occurrence of man among the all of beings. On the other hand, Heidegger does not twist the original meaning of *Dasein* out of all recognition: it does mean primarily the factual existence, the thereness of man in a world. Only, this thereness has to be thought in Heidegger's sense as an event which brings the illumination of being into the world-all, and does so because it is a disclosing way of being. The implications suggested by Heidegger with the word *Dasein* may be unfolded in the following way: When there is man, the "there is . . ." happens; man's factual existence (his being-there) discloses thereness, as the thereness of himself, the thereness of world, and the thereness of beings within the world, some like himself and some unlike himself.

This interpretation of *Dasein* follows Heidegger's own (cf. SZ, pp. 132 ff.), and far from saying too much, it does not nearly exhaust all that Heidegger suggests with this simple and eloquent word. As far as its English translation goes, the nearest approach that can be made is probably "there-being" or "being-there," but the shortcomings of this expression are unhappily many: first and most importantly, it refuses to be eloquent; secondly, it cannot suggest all the meanings required; and thirdly, it is a purely ontological term. While in *Sein und Zeit* the ontological meaning of *Dasein*, as the illuminated-disclosing thereness of being, on the ground of which man exists as man, is undoubtedly by far the most important, the word carries at the same time an ontic meaning: it names the concrete beings we ourselves are. This, in fact, is how Heidegger defines *Dasein* when he first introduces the concept. (Cf. SZ, p. 7.) It is essentially a two-dimensional term, with an ontic-ontological meaning.

It is not surprising that this key word presents a problem to every translator and expositor of *Sein und Zeit*. There seem to be three alternatives open, the first of which is to construct an expression like being-here or being-there. This solution has been rejected in this book, for reasons already stated in the preceding paragraph. Secondly, the German word *Dasein* could be used in the English text. This solution, although in many ways the best, has also been avoided in this book, because of the danger that *Dasein* might become merely a technical term in a Heideggerian terminology, instead of being re-thought and genuinely understood. Thirdly, a familiar English expression, like human being or man could be used, in spite of Heidegger's objections to it. Of these two, human being has the advantage of lending itself to the same ontic-ontological use as *Dasein*: it could mean both a concrete human being and the human way of being. This, however, is offset by several disadvantages, first among them the weakness and lack of character of the expression itself. Further, it defines "being" by the humanity of man, whereas *Dasein* asks us to do exactly the opposite, namely to understand man's humanity from his being. But the decisive consideration is that "human being" presents the almost insoluble linguistic problem whether it should be referred to as he or it. Human being, in an ontological sense, could only be called *it*, whereas it goes against the grain in English to refer to a concrete human being in any other way but as *he*. The same difficulty arises in English with any other two-dimensional expression, which names both man and his being in the same breath.

After weighing up all these alternatives, the following solution was adopted in this book: Where the ontological meaning of *Dasein* is of exclusive or predominant importance, it will be expressed in a way most suitable to the context, e.g. as factual existence, as man's being or being-there or occasionally even as being-here. Mostly, however, preference will be given to the word *man*, a word that commends itself by its simplicity, although Heidegger's objections to it must always be borne in mind. Above all, it must be remembered that *man* is a purely ontic term and is incapable of bringing into play the ontological meaning of *Dasein*. This inadequacy is most acutely felt in the oft-recurring phrase: man exists for the sake of himself. The full meaning of *Dasein* allows, and indeed demands, a very different interpretation of this sentence from the one it suggests at first sight. Man's being-there, the sentence says, is for the sake of thereness; its utmost illumination is gathered in man's own self; this is for the sake of which man exists.

☙§ II The Worldishness of World

1. *The fundamental existential constitution of man: being-in-the-world Heidegger's conception of world*

To exist as a self is man's ownmost possibility, but not by any means the only one fundamental to him. The possibility of relating himself to other beings inseparably belongs to man's existence. Man is indeed so essentially self-relating that his understanding of himself as the primary *for the sake of* already gives him his bearings in a world: it directs him in advance to the things he may meet as the *means by which* something can be done *in order to* accomplish this or that; this, in turn, may do service *for* some purpose, which may be directly or indirectly *for the sake of* a possibility of his own existence. The whole complex of "by means of . . . in order to . . . for . . ." springs from and leads back to man's own being, with which it is disclosed in an original unity. This relational complex forms the coherence-structure of the world, or more precisely, as will be explained presently, of the specific kind of world which Heidegger takes to exemplify the idea of world as such. The way in which man fore-goingly refers himself to . . . , directs himself toward . . . , is the condition of the possibility that in his factual existence he never finds himself in a vacuum as an isolated self, but in the midst of other beings in the coherent whole of a world. The original disclosure of man's own being in a relational-whole constitutes the fundamental structure of his being as being-in-the-world.

The original, indivisible unity of being-in-the-world is taken by Heidegger as the *minimal* basis on which man's being can be explained. In this fundamental constitution, ". . . the-world" does not mean a real connection of real things, but characterizes the unique way in which man understands himself. ". . . the-world" is an existential-ontological concept, which gives no information about any ontic world, but formulates the problem of the possibility of world as such.

At the same time, as Heidegger constantly emphasizes, all ontological concepts must have an ontic basis. If we, in our concrete existence, did not always and, as if it were, by necessity understand ourselves "in a world," the ontological inquiry would remain groundless. The *ontic* concept of world from which Heidegger's analysis starts is that of a world in which a factually existent man "lives." (Cf. SZ, p. 65.) Why Heidegger puts the word "lives" into quotation marks, will become clear later. For the moment, it is more important to note that Heidegger takes for the basis of his inquiry the ordinary, workaday world of everyday existence (*Umwelt*). This eminently practical world, in which things hang together as ends and means, is obviously very different from any theoretical conception of "world" as a causally connected natural universe, as well as from the vaguer concept of a totality of beings, which leaves the nature of the "totality" completely undefined. All these ontic concepts of "world," namely, nature, the natural universe, the all of beings, are decisively rejected by Heidegger, so much so that when he uses the term "world" in any of these senses, he always writes it in quotation marks.

Three different meanings of the term "world" have now been indicated, and, since they must be clearly distinguished in *Sein und Zeit*, the following summary may be found helpful:

1. In the existential constitution of man as being-in-the-world, ". . . the-world" characterizes the way in which man exists. It is an existential-ontological concept.

2. The ontic-existentiell concept of a world in which man "lives," and more specifically, the nearest workaday world of everyday existence (*Umwelt*), forms the basis and starting point of Heidegger's analysis. It is from this world that his concrete illustrations and examples are drawn.

3. The "world," always written in quotation marks in *Sein und Zeit*, means a real connection of real beings, usually understood as nature, or the totality of beings, but sometimes also denoting a more indeterminate whole of things, facts, people, etc. of which we usually imagine the world to be "made up." It must be judged from the context in which of these senses the "world" is to be understood, but in every case the quotation marks should be noted with care, because they draw attention to concepts that not only diverge from Heidegger's, but no longer mean a world at all. According to Heidegger, the phenomenon of world can never be explained from concepts like nature, the universe, the all of beings, etc. because they themselves already presuppose an understanding of world.

On what grounds does Heidegger put forward such an unusual thesis? Let us consider the concept of nature. Difficult as this may be to define, it is evident that nature in the ontic sense is something that is: it belongs to the realm of real beings. Or even when nature is used as an ontological-categorial concept, it can only mean the being, the reality of actual or possible real beings as a whole. Whichever the case may be, certain preconditions must be fulfilled before these real beings can make themselves manifest as the beings they are. The first condition is obviously that they must in some way be accessible to man, that man must be able to meet them in the same world in which he already finds himself. To be able to do so, a world must already be disclosed, and can never be retrospectively "made up" from the things met within it.

The same consideration applies to the concept of a totality of beings. In whatever way the "totality" may be explained, one thing at least is certain: the totality must have a radically different character from a sum total, not only because no conceivable addition could ever arrive at the "total," but because every single thing added together would already have met us in the predisclosed whole of a world. It is evident, therefore, that the world cannot consist of things, nor of things and people added together, because understanding ourselves in a world is the condition of the possibility that we can meet any kind of beings at all. Least of all can the world itself have the character of a real thing. When we ask, "What is world?" we are already blocking the way to a genuine understanding of this phenomenon, because with the "what," we are usually on the lookout for a thing or the essence of a thing. The world is not a thing, but man himself is worldish: he is, at the bottom of his being, world-disclosing, world-forming. Man alone is so, that he fore-goingly, a priori, understands his own being in a relation-whole, in which and from which he can meet other beings and understand them in *their* being.

The disclosure of world thus proves to be an essential constituent of man's understanding of being, and as such belongs to the central problem of *Sein und Zeit*: How is it possible for man to understand being? What does being mean? The fundamental constitution of being-in-the-world is not, as it is sometimes thought to be, an *answer* to Heidegger's question, but is a sharper and fuller formulation of the question to be answered. In this formula, ". . . the-world" is a vast question mark, whose meaning has been briefly indicated in the preceding paragraph, but which must now be more fully explained as follows:

Man, as the finite being he is, cannot himself make the beings he needs, and cannot therefore know anything in advance of their real qualities and properties, which are vital to him for his own existence. Unable to create anything, man must be able to receive what is already there, and not merely anyhow, in an unintelligible jumble of impressions, but in such a way that these things become accessible *as* the things they are, understandable in their being. This is only possible if they can show themselves in a coherent whole, which is not merely an empty frame, like an iron hoop holding a jumble of things together, but is a whole which has a definite structure of its own, so that in it and from it the multitude of beings are in advance understandable in an *articulated* coherence. This structural whole (world), which Heidegger will show to be a complex of references or relations, must enable man to refer himself to other beings in a purposeful way, and, conversely, to relate them to himself in their relevance to and bearing upon his own existence.

The articulated whole of a world, as was indicated above, is always understood by us in advance, and cannot be retrospectively glued together from any number of sense impressions and perceptions of actual things, events, people, etc. On the contrary, if these perceptions did not take place in a previously disclosed whole, any coherent and intelligible experience would be impossible.

The disclosure of world necessarily goes before experience, and one possible explanation is that the world must be "formed" in and with man's own being. Man himself is "world-forming," or, as it may also be expressed, "world-imaging" (*weltbildend,* cf. Grund, p. 39). This "world-image," of course, must not be thought of as a sort of advance copy of a flesh and blood world, but as a wholly insubstantial horizon of meaning, a whole of reference in which we always move with so much familiarity that we do not even notice it. The ontological problem is to show and explain in detail how man himself must be in order to be capable of "fore-imaging" a world to which experience has contributed nothing. This is the *problem* which Heidegger formulates with the fundamental constitution of man as being-in-the-world.*

How does Heidegger propose to solve his problem? What is the basic thought that guides him? It may be summed up in the following thesis: The very finiteness of man makes it both possible and necessary for him to "form" a world. It is because his own being is in advance disclosed to him in its dependence that there lies in it already a disclosing reference to the being of other beings.

This basic thought is clearly hinted at in the reference complex, "by means of . . . in order to . . . for . . . ," which was briefly mentioned in the first paragraph of this chapter. This complex is a simplification of a much more elaborate structure worked out by Heidegger in his world analysis. (Cf. SZ Div. 1, chap. 3.) For our purpose, which is not to follow up

* For the problem of world, as it is posed by Heidegger, a study of his *Kant und das Problem der Metaphysik* is most rewarding. For Heidegger's interpretation of time, Section 35 of this work is especially illuminating.

the details of Heidegger's analysis, but to get an insight into his fundamental idea of world, it is sufficient to grasp that this relational-complex, only more elaborately articulated, forms the structure of world, and it is with its help that man in advance refers himself to . . . , directs himself toward . . . , anything that might appear within his horizon.

For the point we are considering, the "by means of . . ." is especially illuminating: it is in itself a document of man's finite being. If man were a perfect substance, distinguished by independence and self-maintenance without recourse to anything apart from itself, he would not need to refer himself to a thing as the "means by which . . . ." More than that, it would be inexplicable how, as a perfectly self-contained being, he could even understand that something might be needful or useful for accomplishing something else.

It is because man's being is disclosed to him in its jeopardy and dependence that it must in advance refer him to the possibility of meeting other beings and prescribe the ways in which they can bear on his own existence, e.g. by way of dangerousness, usefulness, harmfulness, etc. To solve the problem of world, Heidegger must show in detail how this disclosure takes place and what are those existential structures which are capable of performing the task of disclosure.

Of the basic structures which have a specifically *disclosing* function, Heidegger names three: *Befindlichkeit,* which may be rather inadequately rendered as "attunement"; *Verstehen,* understanding; and *Rede,* speech. The latter will not enter into the discussion at present, and, since it may easily confuse the reader, it should be noted that by "speech" Heidegger does not mean the ontic phenomenon of language, but an existential structure which makes language possible.

The existential concept of *Befindlichkeit* cannot be adequately expressed by any single English word. The common

German phrase, *Wie befinden Sie sich?* means: How do you feel? How are you? *Sich befinden* generally means how one is, how one feels. Important also is the core of the word: *sich finden,* to find oneself. The whole expression may be explained as follows: man is a priori so that his being manifests itself to him by the way he feels; in feeling, he is brought to himself, he finds himself. The ontic manifestations of *Befindlichkeit* are familiar to everyone as the moods and feelings which constantly "tune" man and "tune him in" to other beings as a whole. To avoid having to coin some clumsy expression for *Befindlichkeit,* it is convenient to call it "attunement."

In Heidegger's interpretation, attunement must on no account be taken for a "lower" faculty which is at war with the "higher" faculty of understanding. For one thing, neither attunement nor understanding are faculties, but existentials, i.e. ways of being. Each has its own character and way of disclosing, which is not only not opposed to the other, but is in advance "tuned in" to the other. Attunement always has its understanding; understanding is always attuned. Each has a specific disclosing function in the whole of care.

The moods and feelings, which are apt to be dismissed by us as accidental and meaningless, are ontologically of great importance, because they originally bring man to himself as the factual self he already is. Each mood reveals in a different way, e.g. in joy, man is manifest to himself as he who is enjoying himself; in depression, as he who is weighed down by a burden, etc. Tuned by moods and feelings, man finds himself in his thrown being, in the inexorable facticity "*that* I am and have to be," delivered over to myself to be as I can, dependent upon a world for my own existence.

Moods and feelings rise from man's thrownness and bring him face to face with it. By "thrownness," Heidegger does not mean that man is cast into the "natural universe" by a blind force or an indifferent fate, which immediately abandons him to his own devices, but means: his own "real" existence is manifest to man in the curious way that he can always and only find himself *already* here, and can never get behind this *already* to let himself come freely into being. But although he can never originate his being, yet he is "delivered over to himself": he *has* to take over his being as his. Man's fundamental impotence and dependence, that he cannot make and master his own being, are originally and elementally revealed by attunement.

But moods and feelings tune man not as an isolated self; on the contrary, they bring him to himself in such a way that he finds himself there, in the midst of other beings. With this "in the midst of . . .," man is already lifted into a world, surrounded by beings which are always manifest in a certain wholeness. *Why* this is so cannot yet be shown, but *that* it is so is not an accident; it lies in the structure of attunement itself to refer man to the possibility of other beings as a whole. Moods and feelings, far from being "inarticulate," have a distinctively articulated structure. This can best be demonstrated by Heidegger's analysis of fear as a specific mode of attunement (cf. SZ Sec. 30), which we shall now consider as far as it is relevant to this discussion.

In the mood of fear, three main articulations can be distinguished: "fear of . . .," "fear itself" (fearing, being afraid), and "fear for . . . ."

In fear as "fear of . . ." there lies already a disclosing reference to other beings, which can approach from the world in the character of the fearsome. Fear in advance refers itself to something definite, whether it is another man, or a thing, or an event, which can approach by way of a threat from a definite direction. It should be observed that in fear as "fear of . . ." there must already be disclosed something like a relation-whole, something like a neighborhood, from which some definite thing can approach as the fearsome.

"Fear itself," the fearing (being afraid), discloses the fearsome by opening itself to its fearfulness, by letting its threateningness strike home. It is not that some future evil is first discovered as an objective "fact" and then feared, but fear itself discovers something in its fearsomeness. It is only because man himself is constantly tuned by latent fear that he can "in fact" discover something as threatening. A detached observation and investigation of an object could never find out that it is fearful.

Existential attunement is the condition of the possibility of what Heidegger calls *Angänglichkeit*. *Angänglich* means in the first place: approachable, capable of letting something come near. *Angehen,* as in the phrase, *es geht mich an,* means: it is my business, it is my concern, it touches me, it strikes me, moves me. On the ground of attunement, man is approachable, concernible, touchable, strikable, capable of being affected and moved by . . . whatever may approach him from the world. Man could never be affected through the senses, if attunement did not in advance throw him open to be affected in various ways; for instance, something like resistance could never be discovered by the sense of touch, if man were not in himself already "touchy."

For Heidegger, affection and perception through the senses are not primary, "ultimate" phenomena, but are founded in, i.e. require for their necessary foundation the more original phenomenon of attunement. It is clear also that in Heidegger's interpretation, receptivity through the senses is not a *pure* receptivity, a mere passive soaking up of what is given, but is grounded in the spontaneous activity of attunement, which throws man open and constantly keeps him open to whatever may approach from the world.

The same thought is expressed by Heidegger in the phrases "letting be" (*Seinlassen*) and "letting meet" (*Begegnenlassen*), which constantly meet the reader in *Sein und Zeit* and are often felt to be obscure and confusing. These phrases imply: man's finite being-in-the-world is neither the creativeness of an infinite Being, who can make actual, concrete beings, nor, on the other hand, is it the pure passivity of something made. It is a spontaneously active receiving of what is already there, in the course of which things are set free in their being (*freigeben, Freigabe*); they are delivered from their hiddenness and given the possibility to be disclosed in their being. This disclosure happens when man "throws a world" over things, within which they can show themselves as and for the things they are.

But, as far as our discussion has gone, it is still not clear how the world itself is disclosed, or, to speak more precisely, how man's own being is manifest to him as being-in-the-world. It is true that in Heidegger's hands a mere mood has already revealed more than would have been thought possible, but so far, the "wholeness" of a world has always been presupposed. Let us now turn to fear as "fear for . . ." to see what further light it can throw on our problem, and whether attunement, taken by itself, can make the disclosure of being-in-the-world fully understandable.

Fear is always "fear for . . . ." In being afraid, man is afraid for himself. Man is capable of fear, because in his being it is this being itself which is at stake. The threat to his ability-to-be makes manifest to man his deliverance over to himself. Even when the fear is not directly and immediately for his own being, but for property and possession, man still fears for himself, because his access to things, his "being near to things" essentially belong to his being-in-the-world. Similarly, when a man is afraid for someone else, he still fears also for himself, being threatened in the most fundamental relational possibility of his existence, his being with others like himself (*Mitsein*).

What has this summary of Heidegger's analysis of fear brought to light? What and how does attunement disclose? It discloses man in his existence (self) *as* already thrown into a world, in the midst of other beings, upon which he is dependent. Attunement not only throws man open to the possible thereness (thatness) of other beings, but different moods in advance prescribe *how* their thereness can show itself: joy discovers it as joyful, pleasure as pleasing, fear as fearsome, and so on. Attunement is itself a way of being-in-the-world. It rises from the depth of man's thrownness and reveals, more elementally and far-reachingly than any thinking can overtake, *that* he is and has to be, dependent upon a world and being borne in upon by what might befall him from it.

But although attunement reveals elementally and far-reachingly, it yet fails to illuminate fully the meaning of what it reveals. Attunement itself constantly delivers man over to the beings in the midst of which he finds himself. In his thrownness, man falls captive to his "world"; he is enthralled and bemused by the things that are; he is pressed in upon and hemmed in by them (*benommen*). To achieve freedom of movement and full illumination, man must somehow free himself from his thralldom to what is, he must transcend beings as a whole, among them first and foremost himself. But what is it *to* which man can transcend? He transcends to the *possibilities* of his being. Not from how he is, but from how he can be, does man become transparent to himself as the thrown self he already is.

The disclosure of possibilities *as* possibilities is the achievement of existential understanding. In Heidegger's interpretation, understanding is not a cognitive faculty, like comprehending, explaining, etc. but is a basic way of existing. It is, in fact, nothing other than the "fore-structure" of care, whereby man is constantly before himself, ahead of himself. Since understanding is a structure of the original whole of care, it must necessarily be "tuned" by attunement. All the possibilities of man's being which understanding can disclose must hence be possibilities of a thrown and dependent being as disclosed by attunement. Keeping this important thought in mind, let us now examine in greater detail the "fore-throw" structure of understanding and see how it helps to "fore-form" the relational-whole of world.

Heidegger characterizes understanding as an *Entwurf*. *Entwerfen* means to throw forth, to throw forward and away from oneself: it is basically the same word as *to project*. Similarly, the noun *Entwurf* has the same meaning as a project, something that has been thrown forward, projected. *Entwurf* in the pregnant sense, however, does not mean just any kind of project, like going for a picnic tomorrow, but means the ground plan, the first basic design, the all-embracing conception which in advance encircles the whole and so makes it possible for any detail in it to "hang together," to "make sense." Conversely, the fore-throw of an all-embracing whole has its meaning in referring back to all that it embraces. This gives us a clue to the essentially two-way structure of understanding: it throws forward possibilities, but, at the same time, it holds out *toward* itself what it has fore-thrown. This can be easily tested by us, simply by thinking of some possibilities we are planning to carry out. A little imagination will show that while we throw these possibilities forward, they at the same time turn round and seem positively to look at us.

But the original possibilities which existential understanding throws before and toward itself are not of empirical things and happenings; they are the possibilities of man's being as a whole. They can be a whole only because they are in advance manifest from the possibility of a *not,* which ends all his possibilities and thus in advance closes them. The understanding of this *not* reveals to each man his being as singly and solely his, and so brings him to himself in the uniqueness of his finite self. But this self is already tuned by attunement to find itself dependent upon a world in which and from which the thereness of other beings presses in and bears upon itself. Hence the possibilities of this self must necessarily be of existing-in-the-midst-of . . ., existing-in-relation-to . . . . The fore-throw, in which attuned understanding brings the whole of the possibilities of man's thrown being before itself, is the original happening of being-in-the-world.

In going out beyond all "that" and "there," understanding throws open the horizon of the possibilities of man's being *as the world,* in which man can be a factual self among other beings. Understanding thus throws a world over beings as a whole, among them man himself as he already is (*Überwurf*, cf. Grund, p. 39). The horizon of world is transcendental: it in advance encompasses the whole of man's being. Understanding thus opens up a distance between the factual self man already is and the utmost limit of his possibilities. Only from this distance to himself can man become fully illuminated *as* a self: that he can be himself only and always as the thrown self he already is, referred to beings he has not made and cannot master, but with this essential difference: he can be this self in the mode of flight and covering over, or he can take over his finite possibilities as fully and wholly his own.

It has now become possible to clear up a puzzling question which the reader may already have asked himself: how can a man "disown" himself to the world and yet exist for the sake of himself? The world, as interpreted by Heidegger, is not something apart from man, but is man himself in the whole of his possibilities, which are essentially relational. It is for the sake of these that man exists: the *for the sake of* is the primary and basic character of world. It is from this horizon that things are first opened up in *their* possibilities, i.e. are understood *as* the things they essentially are. The essence of things in our ordinary, everyday world (*Umwelt*) is to be means to ends, because the world-horizon which is primarily "meaning-giving" has the basic character of the *for the sake of* man's own existence.

It has now been shown that an attuned understanding is capable of "fore-forming" a world, which not only precedes experience but is far more than a vague, inarticulate wholeness. Attunement not only throws man open to the being (thatness) of other beings, but in advance prescribes *how* their being is discoverable, e.g. as threatening, as joyful, etc. The understanding fore-throw of man's possibilities of being not only embraces them in advance as a whole, but with the *for the sake of* gives a fore-image of how the things discoverable within it can "hang together," how they can "make sense." The relational complex of "by means of . . . in order to . . . for . . . ," whereby man in advance refers himself to whatever may appear within his horizon, is only possible in an original unity with the *for the sake of*, and constitutes the ontological structure, the worldishness of man's primary and basic world (*Umwelt*).

This structure, however, as Heidegger explicitly remarks (cf. SZ, p. 65), is modifiable into the worldishness of specific "worlds," i.e. there are other ways in which man can relate himself to beings as a whole. It appears, then, that the ontological meaning of the relational structure of world has not yet been fully brought into view, and needs further elucidation.

Heidegger interprets the essentially relational way in which man understands his being as a signifying. The *for the sake of* signifies a *for*; this signifies an *in order to*; this, a *means by which,* etc. Understanding holds out the familiar whole of these relations before and toward itself in an originally disclosed unity, and lets itself be referred by these relations themselves. In his familiarity with these relations, man signifies to himself, gives himself originally to understand how he is and can-be-in-the-world. The relation-whole of this signifying is interpreted by Heidegger as significance. The ontological structure of world, the worldishness of world as such, is significance. (Cf. SZ, p. 87.)

Heidegger's interpretation of the ontological structure of world as a significance-whole makes it understandable that man's primary world can be modified into specific "worlds," by taking other relational complexes as "significant." Moreover, it completely justifies Heidegger's bald refusal to acknowledge any real connection of real things as world in the genuine sense. The coherence of a world made possible by an understanding of significance is of a totally different order from the real connections of things, which persist regardless of whether there is man to discover them or not. If man disappears from the face of the earth, things will not fly off into space but will go on gravitating toward the earth, even though there is no one to discover and understand something like gravity. But the *significant* reference complex "by means of . . . in order to . . . for . . ." obviously cannot persist except insofar as there is man who relates himself to things in this signifying way. Significance, i.e. world, only "is" in the understanding of man, to whom his own being is disclosed as being-in-the-world.

The basic idea which guides Heidegger's interpretation of world was set out earlier in the following thesis: The very finiteness of man makes it both possible and necessary for him to form a world. It is because his own being is disclosed to him in its dependence that there lies in it in advance a disclosing reference to the being of other beings. This thesis has now been elucidated in as much detail as the limits set to this book allow. Has the discussion brought us to the answer to Heidegger's question: how is it possible for man to understand being? Not yet. Some important steps toward it have been taken: it has become evident that the original disclosure of being must happen through attunement, which reveals the "that I am," and that the "fore-imagings" of understanding must already be tuned by this disclosure. But as to the innermost possibility of these events, no explanation has yet been given, nor can Heidegger be expected to give it until the end of his inquiry.

For the present, the most urgent task is to get a more concrete grasp of what has emerged so far. This is all the more important because Heidegger's ideas are far removed from our accustomed ways of thinking, and even when all due allowance has been made for the remoteness of ontological interpretations, it may be rightly felt that these must be relevant to our concrete experience or else be banished into the sphere of abstract speculations. Is there any way in which Heidegger's idea of world can be brought nearer to us? Are there any obstacles which obscure its relevance to our experience and which can be removed at this stage?

There is at least one obstacle which can be easily removed. This lies in the strictness of Heidegger's thought and language, essential to philosophy but unnecessary to our everyday existence, as a result of which we often fail to recognize in what Heidegger says the perfectly familiar experience of our own being-in-the-world. For instance, we usually equate *being* with *living*, so that we rarely think or speak of *being* in a world, but rather of living in, or staying in, or moving in a world of a specific character. We do not, for example, say of a woman that she *is* in her domestic world, but that she *lives* in it. What we mean by this phrase is nevertheless one specific concretization of being-in-the-world in Heidegger's sense: the possibilities of this woman's existence, we imply, are gathered up in family and home, on which she habitually spends herself. She holds out these possibilities before herself *as the world* in which she is at home. It is in and from these possibilities, i.e. from her world, that she understands herself in relation to other beings; and, conversely, it is by reference to her world that she understands other beings in their relevance to and bearing upon her own existence.

This example not only shows the connection between Heidegger's ontological idea of world and the world we "live" in but also helps us to understand one of the most puzzling features of the expression *being-in-the-world.* At first sight, the word "in" almost irresistibly suggests a spatial relation, so that the image formed of the world is that of a vast spatial container in which we occupy an insignificant spot. Heidegger is well aware of this danger, and that is why on introducing the concept of being-in-the-world his first concern is to discuss the meaning of the "in." (Cf. SZ, p. 54.) The word, Heidegger explains, cannot have the same spatial-categorial meaning as it has when we speak of an extended thing being *in* an extended spatial container, ". . . as water is 'in' the glass, as clothes are 'in' the wardrobe." Man cannot be "in space" as an extended thing but only in the way appropriate to himself as being-in-the-world: he discloses space in relating himself to things by way of undistancing them and directing them to . . . . This existential spaceishness is only possible on the ground of, and as an essential constituent of, man's fundamental worldishness. Something like space must, therefore, belong to a world, but it is not primarily, let alone exclusively, constitutive of world. (Cf. SZ Div. 1, chap. 3 B & C.)

That the "in" does not have a spatial-categorial meaning,

was concretely shown by our example: a woman does not live *in* her domestic world by occupying space in it but by keeping herself to these familiar possibilities of her existence. Similarly, we are not thinking of a spatial relation when we say of a man that he moves in the artistic world, or that he is at home in the society world, etc. What Heidegger, in a strictly ontological sense, calls "being-in" is concretely experienced by us as "living-in," or "moving-in," or "being-at-home-in." All these phrases express the same meaning: staying-close-to . . ., being-familiar-with . . ., in-habiting [both in the sense of habituation and dwelling] . . . a world of this or that specific character.

Why is it that the world we "live" in is familiar to us always in this or that specific way? Because our possibilities are essentially finite, not only in the sense that they are in fact limited, but because possibilities in themselves have a not-character. These finite possibilities, moreover, are manifest to each one of us as the possibilities of *my* being; *the* world is therefore always essentially *my* world.

But does this mean that each man is locked into a world of his own from which he may never truly get across to another man's world? Any such thought is obviously alien to Heidegger, to whom the world itself is nothing but the relation-whole in which man understands himself among other beings. Insofar as these other beings are fellowmen, they also are-in-the-world in the same way as himself. Man is not only not locked into a world of his own, but the world is his in such a way that he in advance shares it with others like himself.

Man's relation to other men is shown by Heidegger to be fundamentally different from his relation to things. Being-with others like himself (*Mitsein*) belongs directly to man's existence (self) and helps to constitute its world-forming character, whereas his being-near-to things (*Sein-bei*) is founded upon his thrownness and factual dependence on a world. Man cannot be *with* things in a mutually shared world, because things are only within-worldish (*innerweltlich*); they are discoverable *within* the world, but are unable to disclose their own being *in* a world.

When Heidegger speaks of "world" (nature) in quotation marks, he usually means purely an ontic connection of *things*, because beings who exist as men can never merely occur in nature like things, which have the character of reality. The fundamentally different way in which man relates himself to fellow-existences from the way in which he refers himself to things also helps to explain why Heidegger cannot work out both relations at the same time in his world-analysis. (Div. 1, chap. 3.) The theme of fellow-existences is introduced into the analysis only briefly; its detailed elucidation is left over to a subsequent chapter. (Div. 1, chap. 4.) The ontological structure of world is worked out by Heidegger exclusively from the relation-complex ("by means of . . ." etc.) whereby man refers himself to things. Following Heidegger's own trend, the theme of man's everyday self in relation to other selves will be dealt with separately in this book, after the discussion of world and of the reality of things within the world has been concluded. (Part II, chap. IV of this book.)

Accordingly, we shall at this stage confine our attention to man's being-near-to things, or, as it may also be expressed, his staying-close-to the "world" (*Sein-bei*). How are man's dealings with things characterized by Heidegger? Since man inhabits the world by way of care, each of his fundamental relations must have a specific care-character: he is near to things by "taking care" of them (*besorgen*). "Taking care" is an existential-ontological term whose meaning may be explained as follows: a basic way in which man inhabits his world is to reckon with things, to take account of things. With man's factual existence, his taking care of things splits itself up into an extraordinary variety of ways, of which Heidegger gives a long list of examples: "having to do with something, producing something, preparing and cultivating something, using something, giving up and losing something, undertaking, carrying out, investigating, questioning, observing, discussing, defining . . ." (Cf. SZ, p. 56.) Among the deficient modes of taking care, Heidegger mentions desisting from something, missing (an opportunity), taking a rest, etc.

Man is near to things primarily in a practical way by using and handling them. A deficiency of careful (care-taking) having-to-do-with things makes possible an important modification whereby man's primarily practical approach becomes modified into the only-looking-at things of theory. Although theory, just as much as practice, is a taking care of things, the theoretical approach represents a profound modification of man's original understanding of reality, whose consequences are so far-reaching that it requires a discussion on its own. (See next section of this chapter.)

Before going on to consider theory and practice, however, the main conclusions reached so far may be briefly summarized as follows:

The world is not a thing, nor does it consist of things. The coherent whole of a world cannot be explained from the real connections of real beings but only from the way in which man a priori understands his own being in the whole of its possibilities. These possibilities belong to a finite and dependent being and are hence necessarily relational. They are disclosed by attuned understanding in anticipation of possible other beings. The articulated reference-whole (significance-whole), in which and from which man in advance refers himself to any possible beings he might meet, constitutes the ontological structure, the worldishness of world. It enables man a priori to understand the being of other beings and is disclosed in co-original unity with man's own being as the primary *for the sake of*. On the ground of his fundamental constitution of being-in-the-world, a world essentially belongs to man and its basic character is therefore the *for the sake of*. This prescribes the significance-structure of man's nearest everyday world in which he takes care of things primarily in a practical way by using and having-to-do-with them. This original way of taking care of things is capable of being modified into a theoretical only-looking-at things. In view of the predominantly, if not exclusively, theoretical approach of Greek-Western philosophy and of the positive sciences that have sprung from it, leading ultimately to the present Atomic Age, Heidegger's elucidations of this problem have a much wider than purely philosophical interest.

2. *The theoretical and practical way of taking care of things*

What does Heidegger mean when he characterizes theory as an "only-looking-at" things? Negatively, it must be remarked that the "only" should not be understood in a derogatory sense, although it must be confessed that Heidegger's language would sometimes almost justify such an interpretation. Taken in a strict sense, however, the "only" has a purely ontological meaning. It indicates that something that originally belonged to man's approach to things has been stripped off, leaving the "only-looking" as the dominant and supposedly the only appropriate way to approach them.

What is it that disappears when man's practical having-to-do-with things turns into theory? Is it the making and doing which now give place to observation and thinking? Or is it that the sense of touch and the other senses drop into the background, leaving the sense of vision the predominant role it has undoubtedly played in Greek-Western thinking? There is certainly some truth in these suggestions, but in themselves they cannot explain the difference between theory and practice. As Heidegger points out, it is not even possible to draw a clean demarcation line between "doing" and "thinking," between "touching and handling" and "only-looking-at." (Cf. SZ, p. 358.) A purely practical man, say a small craftsman, may be doing nothing, only looking at his workshop, thinking of the work to be done the next day, the materials to be bought, etc. This looking and thinking are yet purely practical. A theoretician, on the other hand, still uses his tools, if nothing else, paper and pen, not to speak of the elaborate manipulation of instruments that may go into an experiment; yet this doing and handling stand in the service of theory. Heidegger takes great care to emphasize these points, but he still insists on calling theory an only-looking. What is missing from this approach to things, and, in the first place, in what way is theory a "looking" at all?

Theory, Heidegger explains in the lecture "Wissenschaft und Besinnung," comes from the Greek *theorein* and originally means a reverential gazing upon the pure aspect in which a thing shows itself. "Aspect," in this connection, is to be understood in the Greek sense of the *eidos, idea,* the form in which something shows what it is, i.e. its essential being. Theory in the highest philosophical sense means a gazing upon the truth, which takes the truth into its keeping and guards it. (Cf. V/A, p. 53.)

Theory thus turns out to be the same as, or closely akin to, the apprehending, the "seeing," which has of old been called *noein,* the pure, nonsensuous apprehension of beings in their being. This has been traditionally regarded as the only proper ontological approach to things. Why, then, is it an "only-seeing"? What is missing from it that makes it radically different from the practical way of "seeing" things? It is nothing less than the world. The things that are originally understood as belonging to a world and having their place within it are now stripped of their boundaries; they no longer meet man in the horizon of the primary *for the sake of*, but in an indifferent world-all, a natural universe, where they occur in space as purely substantial bodies. Theory is an only-looking which strips things of their world-character and objectivizes them into mere material substances to be found somewhere in an indifferent universal space. (Cf. SZ, pp. 358 ff.; also p. 112.)

The incalculable importance of this fundamental modification in man's understanding of things is that it is from things as mere substances that Greek-Western philosophy takes its start. The consequences of this start for Western science and technology are a constantly recurring theme in Heidegger's later works and deserve serious study. In *Sein und Zeit*, however, the ontological theme predominates, and this is our concern at present.

What are the philosophical consequences of the theoretical start from things as pure substances? The first and most decisive consequence is that the world, in Heidegger's sense, is passed over from the beginning and cannot become even a problem. Nature, the all of beings, is substituted for the genuine phenomenon of world, giving rise to perennial problems of cognition and knowledge, for whose solution countless "theories of knowledge" have been constructed.

Traditional problems of cognition, Heidegger points out, have their source in an insufficient interpretation of man's being. (Cf., e.g. SZ, pp. 59 ff.) The puzzle which hosts of theories of knowledge set out to explain is how a supposedly isolated self, a subject, can get out from his "inner sphere" to an object, the "world" outside himself. But, as Heidegger shows, the completely unjustifiable assumption on which all these theories are based is that man is first of all a "worldless subject" who has subsequently to transcend himself in order to take up a relation to his object, the "world." In Heidegger's interpretation, on the contrary, man is never worldless, and the world is not an object to which he has to "get out." Man *is* so that his own being is in advance manifest to him in a significant relation-whole (world), in which and from which he directs himself toward . . . , relates himself to . . . whatever specific beings he may meet. Only this a priori worldishness of man makes it possible for him to "take up relations" to things in a secondary and derivative way, e.g. in *explicitly* investigating and explaining them, in widening and developing knowledge in various directions, etc.

It is the world-forming character of man's being that is presupposed in all theories of knowledge which take their start from the "subject-object relation" as the supposed "ultimate" that cannot be further elucidated. According to Heidegger, on the contrary, it is precisely this "subject-object relation" that demands a fundamental inquiry, so that its inner possibility can be brought to light. All problems of cognition lead back to the existential constitution of man as being-in-the-world from which they originally spring and on the basis of which alone they can be solved. A deeper inquiry, it is true, will reveal that even this fundamental constitution is insufficient fully to define man's being, but it is the structure from which the analysis and interpretation must start.

Accordingly, the whole of Division One of *Sein und Zeit*, except for one introductory chapter, consists of an analysis of the fundamental constitution of man as being-in-the-world, leading toward an exposition of man's being as care. It has already been shown, however, that man never is-in-the-world in a vague generality but exists always in one or another of the definite modes or manners (*Seinsart*) possible for him. In the first place and for the most part, man exists in the everyday manner of taking care of his "world." The full theme of Division One can therefore be defined as being-in-the-world in the mode of everydayness. The ontic world from which Heidegger's analysis starts is the nearest workaday world of everyday existence (*Umwelt*), and this now requires some further consideration.

3. *The ontic basis of the ontological inquiry into world: the* Umwelt *of everyday existence. The meaning of* Umwelt

The term *Umwelt,* together with two other key words, *Umgang* and *Umsicht,* has so essential a meaning in Heidegger's world-analysis that it well deserves a short discussion on its own.

It is not by accident that each of these key words begins with *Um.* This word is already familiar to us as the *for* of *for the sake of.* A second meaning of *Um* now appears for the first time: it indicates the spatial relation of round-aboutness, nearness, in the sense of immediate surroundings. From what we have learned so far, it is evident that for Heidegger the primary meaning of *Um* is *for,* but, since something like space essentially belongs to a world, the secondary meaning of round-aboutness must also prove to be relevant.

We shall first consider *Umwelt* in its secondary meaning, because this is how in ordinary usage the word is generally understood. Accordingly, *Umwelt* means a world that is round-about us, a world that is nearest, first at hand. There is no appropriate single word in English for *Umwelt*. For most purposes, it can be quite adequately rendered by "environment," but this rendering will not be adopted here. Owing to its biological and sociological flavor, "environment" seems alien to Heidegger's thought and might perhaps with advantage be reserved for an ontology of life, where the "world" of plants and animals could fittingly be called environment or surroundings.

One suggestion which Heidegger undoubtedly intends to convey with *Umwelt* is of a world that is closest and most familiar to man, a world in which he in the first place and for the most part lives. In the absence of an appropriate translation, we shall paraphrase *Umwelt* by "the first and nearest world." It becomes immediately evident how excellently Heidegger's "exemplary" world has been chosen; it is, in a sense, a universal world, since no matter in what age or society, or under what particular conditions a man may live, he cannot, as it were, bypass a world that is first and nearest to him.

For his own illustrations, it is true, Heidegger goes by preference to the world of the small craftsman, but this is only because a small workshop is peculiarly suitable for demonstrating all the essential feaures of man's everyday world. For instance, the reference complex of "by means of . . . in order to . . . for . . ." can be vividly shown by the use of tools on the work in progress; "nature" enters as the source of materials needed for the work; the "others" are also there as the merchant who delivers the materials or the customer for whom the clothes, the shoes, etc. are "made to measure"; with the others, the common, public world is also indicated. For purposes of illustration, the little world of the craftsman could hardly be bettered; but it would be a complete misunderstanding to think that Heidegger has only this specific type of world in mind. All that essentially belongs to man's nearest world must be the same regardless of class or age or social-economic developments; its significance-structure must be the same regardless of whether anything is produced in it or not: we only need to think, for instance, of the world of the "idle rich" or of the bedridden invalid.

There is, moreover, a definite way in which man in his everyday existence inhabits his world, and this is what Heidegger calls *Umgang*: man *goes about* the world and *goes about* his business with the things he meets within it. *Umgang* basically means the practical, using and handling way of taking care of things, whose difference from a theoretical only-looking-at things has already been indicated. It must not be thought, however, that the practical having-to-do-with things is blind: it has its own way of "seeing," i.e. of understanding, which Heidegger calls *Umsicht,* meaning literally, *looking around, circumspection.*

Having taken the *Um* in its spatial sense, the three key words have now come into view as: the *world round-about us,* (the first and nearest world); *going about* the world and *about* our practical business with things; *looking around, circumspection.* Suggestive as all this is in itself, what Heidegger intends to say comes fully to light only when we turn to the *Um* in its primary sense of *for.*

Man's first and nearest world is evidently the for-world, in the strict sense that the form, the "how" of its coherence is given by the *for the sake of* his own existence. This prescribes the character of significance, the specific for-worldishness of the everyday world, by the relational complex "by means of . . . in order to . . . for . . . ." Man inhabits his nearest for-world by going about his business in it: his going about is *for* something, whether the something is directly for his own sake, or for the sake of others or whether it is in order to achieve something else to be taken care of. Man's going about his business *for* something is in advance guided by a circumspect for-sight, which discovers what things are *for*, under what circumstances they can be used as means. What circumspect for-sight has "its eye on" in advance is the primary world-form of *for the sake of*, with which the whole significance-structure of "by means of . . . in order to . . . for . . ." is disclosed in an original, indivisible unity.

With the concept of circumspect for-sight, Heidegger gives an existential-ontological explanation of what is familiar to us as *common sense*. The man of common sense sees things in advance in the light of their possible utility, harmfulness, relevance or irrelevance to circumstances. The common-sense view is only possible on the basis of an existential understanding, which fore-throws the possibilities of man's existence *as his world*, in the "light" of which alone the possibilities of things in their relevance to . . . , their bearing upon . . . this or that situation become understandable.

But now the inevitable question arises: Is this everyday understanding of things not merely "subjective"? Is the only-looking of theory not truer, because it is more "objective"? These questions will be dealt with in the next chapter, where the reality of beings within the world will be our theme.

☙ III The Reality of Beings Within the World

The preceding chapters have already shown that reality has a much more restricted meaning in *Sein und Zeit* than in traditional ontologies. Not only man's being is taken out of the sphere of reality but also all existential phenomena, such as, for instance, time and world. These only "are" when a disclosure of being happens. There is one phenomenon of a rather ambiguous character, however, which requires some consideration, and this is language. The existential foundation of language is, indeed, obvious, and yet it is readily overlooked. The reason is that the words of a language can be collected and preserved in books, in which they acquire a certain reality within the world; they become accessible just like things. Hence the impression easily arises that language consists of word-things to which meanings are added. The truth, according to Heidegger's interpretation, is exactly the opposite: man's factual existence discloses world as a significance-whole that can be articulated into those "significances" for which words grow. (Cf. SZ, Sec. 34, esp. p. 161.)

The sphere of reality is thus restricted by Heidegger to

those beings that are independent of a disclosure of being, e.g. plants, animals, the earth, the seas, the stars, etc. All these real things, with their ontic properties and connections, are independent of the disclosure that happens with man's existence: they are there, regardless of whether they are discovered or not. Their being, their reality, on the other hand, is only understandable to man and can never be independent of his existence.

But, as we have seen, things can be approached and discovered in different ways. The two main possibilities we have considered are the practical and the theoretical approach, and of these two, Heidegger maintains, the practical is primary, while the theoretical is secondary and derivative. Things are originally discovered and understood in their reality by the circumspect for-sight of everyday care. This discovers things not as mere substances that happen to be there in a universal space but as utensils that are handily there within the world. Reality thus shows itself in the first place not as the substantial presence of indifferent things but as the handy presence of useful things. The ontological character of the things that meet us within the everyday world is handiness (*Zuhandenheit*).

But, it may be objected, even granted that Heidegger is right in saying that we first understand the reality of things as handiness, these things must already be there in nature before man ever comes on the scene. Are metaphysics and the sciences, each in its own way, not objectively truer, do they not come nearer to things as they are in themselves, just because they understand them in their substantial reality? Is handiness, after all, not merely a subjective coloring we impose on things?

These objections may be briefly answered in the following way: It is certainly true, Heidegger would say, that things must already be there for us to find, otherwise we could never find them. But this is not the point in question. The point is how it is possible for us to understand the "being there" of things at all. We primarily understand that things are handily there, not for any accidental or arbitrary reasons, but because they can become accessible in their being only within a world. Everyday care understands the being of things from their relevance (*Bewandtnis*) to a world, and this is the way in which they can be discovered as they are "in themselves." It is quite erroneous to think that handiness is a "subjective coloring" we cast over things: it is a mode of being prescribed by the significance-structure of world, which enables us to understand things as they are "in themselves." Our everyday having-to-do-with things could never decree the apple tree to be handy if it were not "in itself" handy, at hand, and if its fruit were not "in itself" handy for eating. It is only from long tradition and habit of thought that we almost automatically dismiss what we call "merely subjective" as untrue. If we could not discover things "subjectively," i.e. if we could not let them touch us, concern us, be relevant to us, we could not discover them at all.

Only on the basis of the already discovered handiness of things does their merely substantial presence become accessible. The change from the one to the other comes about by a break in the intimate, completely taken-for-granted reference complex, from which things are understood as things for . . . . Owing to this break, man takes a new look at things, which now show themselves as merely substantial things of such and such qualities and properties. It is only now that the mere whatness of things comes to the surface and hides what they are for. With this change, things are cut off from the *for the sake of*, by reference to which they were originally understood *as* utensils; they "fall out of the world," they become unworlded (*entweltlicht*), and now present themselves as mere products of nature occurring in an indifferent universal space. (Cf. SZ, Secs. 16 and 69.) The traditional idea of being, drawn from this secondary mode of reality, may therefore be called *substantial reality*, as against the *handy reality* of things that belong to a world (*Vorhandenheit*, as against *Zuhandenheit*).

That this is how we *in fact*, though not in theory, understand the things we use in our everyday world is shown by our propensity to ascribe all kinds of "values" to them. The simplest utensil—a knife, for instance—cannot be grasped in its being as a merely substantial thing. The knife is essentially "more" than a material body of such and such properties, of such and such appearance, size, weight, etc. It is this "more" we try to explain when we ascribe a "usefulness value" to the knife. What happens, in fact, is this: standing, as we do, in a long ontological tradition, we unquestioningly take it for granted that the knife is merely substantially real, thereby covering over our original understanding of its being as relevant to . . . , handy for . . . . We first strip the thing bare of what belongs to it as a utensil, then try to restore what we have taken away by adding to it a value.

But, it may be asked, does Heidegger's interpretation not apply only to man-made utensils? These, admittedly, are "more" than mere substances, but what about the material bodies which are simply there in nature? These also, according to Heidegger, are originally understood by us in their handy-being. What, for instance, could be more handily there than the sun, and what could be less man-made? It is not primarily our labor that makes things into utensils; it is the significance-structure of our world that enables us to understand things *as* utensils. Only on the ground of this understanding are we able to improve on what we find, and so make tools that are even handier, even more "valuable" for some specific purpose.

As to the philosophical concept of values, and the elaborate theories of values which have been worked out in the modern era of philosophy, these are considered by Heidegger to be highly questionable and rootless phenomena. They have arisen because the existential constitution of being-in-the-world, on the ground of which man in advance understands the things he meets as "valuable," i.e. handy for something, has been completely overlooked. Once the original whole of being-in-the-world has been passed over, philosophy finds itself compelled to try to glue it together from bits and pieces, by superimposing values on the substances that have fallen out from the significance-whole of a world, just as it is obliged to construct ingenious theories to explain the commerce between a supposedly worldless subject and a cognized "world."

Why is it that in Greek-Western thinking so fundamental a structure as being-in-the-world has been overlooked, and with it the primary ontological character of things as *handy reality* has been consistently missed? It cannot be an accident, nor a failure on the part of the great thinkers of this tradition. The reason lies in the fundamental "fallenness" of man's being, whereby he is whirled away from himself to the things within the world. Instead of interpreting them from his understanding of being-in-the-world, man tries to understand his own being from their reality.

The elemental trend toward the "world" which carries man away from himself cannot fail at the same time to affect the relation most essential to him: his being with other men in a mutually shared world. The radical difference between being-with others and being-near-to things was pointed out already in earlier discussions, and our next task is to examine in some detail Heidegger's ideas on this important theme.

◆§ IV Being-with Others and Being-oneself*

1. *The basic concept of being-with*

Man is able to relate himself to his fellowmen only because his own being is in advance disclosed to him as being-with. This fundamental structure of man's self is the existential foundation of all that we usually speak of under the title of personal relations and human society. If, as a matter of common experience, a man constantly enters into all kinds of associations with other men, this is not the result of the "fact" that he is not the only one of his kind in the world, but the other way round: he *can* recognize others like himself in the world and enter into relations with them because his own being is disclosed to him as being-with. When there are "in

* This chapter seeks to elucidate one of the most widely known themes of *Sein und Zeit,* as it is presented in Div. 1, chaps. 4 and 5 B. In view of the great interest of the theme itself and Heidegger's treatment of it, special care has been taken to follow his text as closely as possible, bringing to the reader, if only in a summarized form, as many passages from it as could be considered within the limits of this book.

fact" no others, when a man is alone, he does not thereby cease to-be-with others, and this fundamental character of his being manifests itself with peculiar intensity in his loneliness, in his missing the others. Even when a man thinks he does not need the others, when he withdraws from them and has nothing to do with them, this is still only possible as a privative mode of being-with.

To our usual way of thinking, it seems the most obvious fact that a man *can* understand others in their being, both as like himself and as other than himself. Ontologically, this fact is a problem which is neither obvious nor easy to explain. In Husserl's phenomenological school, to which at one time Heidegger also belonged, the solution of this problem was thought to lie in "empathy" (*Einfühlung*), literally: "feeling oneself into another." Heidegger rejects this solution, because it assumes that the other is "analogous" to oneself, is a "double" of oneself, and leaves unexplained precisely the most difficult problem: how is it possible that this "double" of myself is yet manifest to me as the "other"? (Cf. SZ, pp. 124 f.)

This is the problem to which Heidegger offers the solution of *being-with*. Just as man is never a worldless subject, but in advance refers himself to the possible presence of things within a world, so he is never an isolated, otherless "I," but in advance understands himself as I-myself-with-(possible other selves). The "with" already refers him to the other as a self, i.e. as one who exists in the same way as he himself and yet is the "other" *with* whom he can be together in the same world.

The basic structure of being-with cannot be reduced to or explained from anything else. The articulated whole of being-myself-with-(another-self) cannot be melted down into an "inarticulate," isolated "I," which then somehow finds its way to another, equally isolated "I." Man does not have to find his way to another man, because with the disclosure of his own being as being-with, the being of others is already disclosed and understood. It is true that in everyday being-together-with-others, this primary understanding of the other, as well as of oneself, is often covered over and distorted, so that to know each other requires a "getting-to-know-each-other." Necessary and unavoidable as such special and explicit efforts may be to disclose one self to another self, they do not originally constitute being-together-with-each-other but are only possible on the ground of the primary being-with.

Being-with others is a basic structure of each man's self, for the sake of which he exists: man therefore exists essentially for the sake of others. He understands them in advance as the selves who are in the world in the same way as himself: their being has the same character of *for the sake of* as his own. On the ground of the irreducible with-structure of his being, man is essentially with-worldish. His world is in advance a world he shares with others; his being-in-the-world is in itself a being-with-others-in-the-world.

But just because being-with is a fundamental constituent of man's own self, it can be modified according to the basic possibilities of existence, i.e. man *can* be with others in an "owned" or a "disowned" way. These possibilities are first hinted at by Heidegger when he introduces the concept of "care-for," as the way of care appropriate to being-with other existences in a mutually shared world. (Cf. SZ, pp. 121 ff.) The meaning of this specific way of care has now to be briefly considered.

"Care-for" is a literal translation of Heidegger's word, *Fürsorge,* and is adopted here to preserve the connection with care and taking-care, but the German word, it should be noted, has a range of meaning which is much better conveyed by the translation in *Being and Time* as *solicitude.* Another way to suggest the general meaning of *Fürsorge* would be to render it by *charity* (*caritas*). Social charitable institutions, Heidegger remarks immediately after introducing his concept of *Fürsorge,* are grounded in the existential care-for, and the need for them is made urgent by the deficient and indifferent ways in which men care for each other in much of their everyday being-together. Passing-by-on-the-other-side and being-of-no-concern-to-each-other are the indifferent modes in which everyday care-for usually keeps itself. But, it should be observed, even the most indifferent way of being-with others is still another order of being from the simultaneous occurrence of a number of objects together.

As to the positive modes of caring-for, Heidegger shows that there are two extreme possibilities; and in these, the owned and disowned way of being-with others comes to light. (Cf. SZ, p. 122.) On introducing this topic, Heidegger treats it with a brevity which seems surprising, until it is realized that it cannot be made genuinely understandable without the interpretation of owned existence which is to follow some two hundred pages later.

In the first of its positive modes, care-for, so to speak, "jumps in" (*einspringen*) for the other; it takes the "care" off the other, usually by taking care of things for him. In so doing, however, it throws the other out of his place by stepping in in his stead, so that the other takes over ready-made what he should have taken care of for himself. In such caring-for, the other can easily become dependent and dominated in such unobtrusive fashion that it may often pass unnoticed by him. This mode of caring-for is widespread in everyday being-together and concerns primarily the handy things that have to be taken care of.

In its second positive mode, care-for, so to speak, "jumps

ahead" (*vorausspringen*) of the other in his ability to be himself, not to take the "care" off him but to give it back to him properly, as his own. Such caring-for is not primarily concerned with what the other does but with his existence as a self, and it may help to make him transparent to himself in his own being as care.

Between these two extremes, there is a wide range of varied and mixed modes of caring-for, whose discussion, as many readers of *Sein und Zeit* note with some regret, is not essential to Heidegger's central theme and is consequently passed over. Instead, Heidegger turns to give a brief indication of the way of "seeing," i.e. of understanding, by which care-for is guided. Parallel to the circumspect for-sight (*Umsicht*) which guides everyday taking-care, care-for has its own ways of "seeing"; these are called by Heidegger *Rücksicht* and *Nachsicht*.

The usual meaning of *Rücksicht* is considerateness, or, if the "seeing" (*Sicht*) is to be emphasized, it might be rendered as a *considerate regard* for someone. *Nachsicht* is excellently rendered in *Being and Time* as *forbearance*. Both these concepts are highly suggestive and could be interpreted in several ways, especially since Heidegger gives no further explanation of their precise meaning. There are, however, some illuminating comments on *Rücksicht,* and its extreme deficiency, ruthlessness, to be found in Heidegger's essay on Anaximander (cf. Ho, pp. 331 ff.), but to discuss these would lead us too far away from our theme.

The interpretation to be given here keeps in view that the concepts under consideration are analogous to *Um-sicht,* for-sight. The first component of *Rück-sicht* means "back-"; *Rücksicht* therefore means an understanding which lies in looking back. What does this understanding look back on? On thrownness and dependence upon a world which has to be taken care of. But thrownness is in itself a thrownness-with and for other; the world has to be taken care of with and for the other. This "back-looking" understanding is evidently the guide of the "jumping-in" mode of caring-for.

Nach-, means after, toward, to; *Nachsicht* is accordingly an understanding that lies in looking toward or to something. What does this understanding look to? To the possibility of being a self, for the sake of which man bears his being as care. But to be a self is only possible with another self. Man thus bears care for the other self; in looking to this, he may help the other to bear his own self as care. This forbearing looking-to the other self is evidently the guide of the "jumping-ahead" way of caring-for.

Both these ways of "seeing" are capable of a wide range of modifications, of which the ruthless disregard of the other's thrownness is an extreme form of deficiency. The indifferent mode of forbearance is called by Heidegger *Nachsehen*. This is not a looking-to, but an overlooking of the other self, a taking-no-notice-of-it; it is not genuine forbearance, but an un-caring toleration, which largely guides the indifferent modes of everyday being-together.

Ultimately, however, all modes of being-together, whether genuine or not genuine, whether they spring from an owned or disowned existence, are made possible by the structure of being-with, which is constitutive of each man's self and which cannot be ironed out so as to leave an undifferentiated identity called an "I." It is because traditional philosophy has always had a worldless, otherless "I" in view that it has been forced to interpret the essence of man, his self, as though it were a substance: a recognizable identity which underlies (is present to) a constantly changing stream of experience.

As against the traditional attempts to explain the self with the help of an idea of being drawn from the reality of things,

Heidegger takes the idea of being-with-others-in-the-world as the only basis from which an ontological analysis of man can even start. This fundamental constitution is not merely a rigid framework, but it itself determines the way in which man is together with others, and even the way in which he himself is a self. In the first place and for the most part, man is captivated and taken in by his world (*benommen*). Hence it comes about that his first meetings with others have a predominantly worldish character: the others meet him in their occupations in the world, of which he himself is also taking care. How does this meeting concretely take place and how does it determine the way in which both the others and one's own self first become understandable?

In his everyday existence, man stays predominantly in his nearest world, in which the others are also busy in their caretaking worldishness. The others are there not merely accidentally, and in addition to what one does with things, but are there in one's occupations from the start, as, for example, the customer for whom the clothes and shoes are "made to measure"; as the merchant who delivers the materials for the work; as the friend who gave a present of the book one reads; the field along which one walks shows itself as owned by so and so, decently cultivated by him, etc. (Cf. SZ, pp. 117 f.)

The others meet us not only in our "private" occupations but also in the common with-world; e.g. in the use of public means of communications; in undertakings which take care in common of the mutually shared world, as in the upkeep of the facilities provided by a community, etc. To an overwhelming extent, everyday being-together does not get beyond the business pursued in common and beyond the average understanding of the others and of oneself which grows from what they do and from what oneself does in the world.

In his average everydayness, man finds the others in their

care-taking being-in-the-world and finds *himself among them* as taking care with them. (Cf. SZ, p. 118.) Far from being an encapsulated I who has to go "out" of himself to another I, man first finds even himself in coming back to himself from "out there," where he is busy taking care of the world among the others. In this common absorption in the world, the "I myself" is not even clearly differentiated from all the other selves; the others are those among whom I also am, among whom I also find myself. In his self-forgetful everydayness, man is in the first place and for the most part not himself.

What does Heidegger mean by the startling announcement that, in his everyday existence, man *is not himself*? Negatively, he clearly cannot mean that man suddenly loses his I-character and ceases to be a self altogether; he can only mean that man exists as a self in *one* of the definite ways that are open to him. How this way of not-being-oneself is to be positively understood will become clear in the next section, where we shall consider Heidegger's answer to the question: *who* is the self of everydayness?

2. *The everyday self and the "they"*

The most salient point which has emerged from Heidegger's analysis can be briefly stated as follows: In the everyday world, the others meet us as *what* they are in their makings and doings: ". . . they *are* what they do." (Cf. SZ, p. 126.)

What Heidegger emphatically says in the sentence, ". . . they *are* what they do," seems at first sight easy to understand. When someone asks us, "Who is so and so?" we almost automatically reply, "he is a surgeon, a businessman, a student of philosophy," etc. But, when we come to think of it, is this habit easy to explain just because it is familiar? Is it so "natural" that the self each man is should be manifest to us from his profession? How is it possible for us to characterize a man's self from what he does? This is the question Heidegger goes on to answer in the paragraph which immediately follows the sentence ". . . they *are* what they do"—a short paragraph which is not only the decisive step taken in the present analysis but is one of the key passages of *Sein und Zeit,* and, as such, is not fully comprehensible where it stands. It is only about halfway through Division Two that this passage will retrospectively come to clarity. Meantime, let us see how far we can understand at present the existential-ontological explanation Heidegger gives of "who's who" in the everyday world.

In the first place, how does man understand himself *as* a self at all? Primarily, as has been shown in our discussion of existence, from the *possibilities* of his being. These are originally manifest from the possibility of a *not,* which belongs to each man singly and uniquely. In the finiteness of his being, each man is sheerly uninterchangeable; no one can stand in for him there, no one can take his being off him and bear it for him. But in everyday being-together, man turns away from the possibility which is most his own and understands himself from his worldish possibilities among other selves. In his everydayness, man in advance measures his own self by what the others are and have, by what they have achieved and failed to achieve in the world. He thus understands himself in his difference from the others by the *distance* which separates his own possibilities from theirs. "Everyday being-together," Heidegger says, "is disquieted by the care for this distance." (Cf. SZ, p. 126.) Everyone measures his distance and so "stands off" as himself from the others. This existential "stand-offishness" (*Abständigkeit*) can concretize itself in many different ways. It is there, for instance, in the care to catch up with the others, to "do as the Joneses do." Or it may manifest itself in the opposite way, in going all out to consolidate some privilege or advantage one has gained and so keep the others down in their possibilities. All kinds of social distinctions, whereby man understands his own existence by his distance from others in class, race, education, income, etc. are grounded in the existential stand-offishness, which means: in the first place and for the most part, man understands his existence by "standing off" from the others and not by the genuine possibilities which lie in the uniqueness of his finite self. In his everydayness, man looks away from the true distance, the limit of his finite being, from which alone he can become truly transparent as the self he is, and measures his self in advance by his distance from what the others are and do.

This existential stand-offishness implies that in everyday existence man draws the possibilities of his being from what is prescribed and decided on by others. He is thus delivered over to the domination (*Botmässigkeit*) of the others and disburdened of the being which is singly and solely his. In everyday being-together, man "*is not* himself; the others have taken his being off him." (Cf. SZ, p. 126.) But who are the others? They are not this one or that one, not anybody or the sum of all: "they" are just "people," the people of whom we say "people think so," and "people don't wear that any more." We call them "they" and "people" to hide that we essentially belong to them, not by what we in fact think and do but in being as we are, measuring the possibilities of our own existence from what "they" say one can be and do.

Since in everyday being-together, "they," the others, are not any definite others, they are essentially interchangeable; anyone can stand in for everybody else, anybody can represent and substitute anyone else, almost like a thing which can just as well represent its genus and species as any other thing. With this, the ontological character of man's being, which is always singly and uniquely *my* being, comes into a mode of not-being in the sense that it *is not* itself according to its ownmost possibility. This is the strictly ontological meaning of Heidegger's thesis that in his everyday being-in-the-world, it *is not* man himself who *is there,* but it is "they," people, who *are there,* oneself among them. In the first place and for the most part, the *who* of everydayness, the everyday self, is the "they" (*Das Man*).

Because of their interchangeability, it is in principle impossible to pin down who "they" are to any definite persons. It is precisely in their inconspicuousness that "they" exercise a dictatorship which can never be brought home to anyone, so that no one can be made responsible for it. There are many social-historical forms in which the dictatorship of "them" can concretize itself. It would be a complete misundersanding of the existential-ontological idea of a "they-self" to think that it applies only to modern society in some specific political-social forms. If Heidegger is right at all in saying that to exist as a they-self is one of the possibilities of man's finitely free being, then this possibility is open to man by virtue of his own being and not by the accident of this or that form of society.

Indeed, no specific oppression is needed to establish the power of "them," because the tendency to level down and average out the distinctiveness of each self is there already in being-together-in-the-world. The reduction to uniformity happens simply in taking care of a mutually shared world, e.g. in using its public facilities, newspapers, entertainments, etc. Here everybody is like everybody else. The existential tendency to average out and level down all differences is commented on by Heidegger in the words: "Everything original is leveled down overnight into the commonplace. Every hard-won achievement becomes small change. Every secret loses its power." (Cf. SZ, p. 127.)

How and why this happens, Heidegger goes on to explain in this way: Stand-offishness, averaging-out and leveling-down constitute the "publicity" of an average understanding of being (*Öffentlichkeit*). This public understanding in advance leads and determines all explanations of self and world, not because it goes deeply into things but, on the contrary, because it is insensitive to differences of genuineness and *niveau*. In this average, public understanding, everything becomes accessible and commonplace, and no one is responsible for having made it so: it is "they" who have understood and decided how things must be. "They" thus disburden everyday existence of responsibility, for "they" are strictly speaking *nobody*, who could be taken to account for anything said and done; it is always the "others" who have said and done so. In everyday being-together, "everyone is the other and no one is himself." (Cf. SZ, p. 128.)

It is in "them," who are nobody, that the everyday self finds its first stability (*Ständigkeit*): it stands as not-itself. This "standing," of course, is not the sheer lastingness of a thing. Although scattering himself into a they-self, man can never become a pure "what"; even to-be-not-himself and nobody is still only possible to a self.

"They" must therefore never be thought of as a genus of which each everyday self is a sample but as a basic way in which man *can* exist as a self. It is for the sake of the they-self that man in the first place and for the most part exists. This primary *for the sake of* articulates the significance-whole of the world in which a man lives and prescribes the average possibilities of being-in-the-world. But just because these possibilities are understood from what "they" are and do, the everyday self covers over its own unique character. It is from the average, public understanding of being that traditional ontology took its start and has been consistently misled by it to ascribe to man's essence, his self, the ontological character of a substance.

The "owned" self of a resolutely disclosed existence is not a different order of being, not some exception or genius that hovers over "them," but is a modification of "them," a resolute gathering of one's self from its scatteredness into a they-self. "They" are a fundamental existential and not some ontic quality of man produced by external conditions. Even less are "they," as is often thought, a contemptible figure of ridicule, although, it must be confessed, Heidegger's language in speaking of the they-self would sometimes almost justify such a conclusion. As against this, Heidegger's own ontological tendency must be held fast. Properly considered, indeed, "they" are far from ridiculous, but a more shattering document of man's finite being than the "owned" self of a resolutely disclosed existence can ever be.

3. *The publicity of everydayness*

a) SPEECH AND LANGUAGE. EVERYDAY SPEECH AS HEARSAY

The theme of the present discussion is the publicity or public disclosedness of everyday being-together, insofar as it is constituted by speech and language. It has already been mentioned that, in Heidegger's interpretation, speech (*Rede*) is a fundamental existential which is co-original with attunement and understanding. These latter have in themselves a definite and intricate structure, so that the being disclosed by them is always already articulated. What is understandable is therefore always expressly articulable. Speech, as an existential, is the articulation of understandability: of existence and fellow-existence, of the significance-whole of world and of the being of beings within the world. Hearing, listening and being silent essentially belong to speech and make up its full ontological structure. Man hears not because he has ears; he has these organs of hearing because by virtue of his own being he is a hearer. Hearing, listening and being silent are existential possibilities that belong to man as a speaker. A stone cannot speak and therefore cannot be silent.

On the ground of his existential constitution, the factually existing man always "speaks out," and it is this "spoken out" speech which Heidegger interprets as the ontic phenomenon of language. It may well be seen from this that the actual languages we have cannot be those "ultimates" for Heidegger from which all explanations have to start. Such an undertaking is all the less feasible because each language already hides in itself one definite explanation (*Auslegung*) of what it articulates, an explanation which is usually so unobtrusive that it remains unnoticed. So, for instance, each language loosens up the significance-whole of world into "significances," which explain in a specific way the everyday world in which man is together with "them," the others.

In everyday being-together, the spoken-out speech, i.e. language, has the character of a communicating talk, whose function is to share with the listener the disclosedness of the things talked about. The listener himself is thus brought into a disclosing relation to the things which are the subject matter of the talk.

Since, however, language itself already gives a certain explanation of the world, it is in itself understandable. In everyday talking-together, there is a strong tendency on the part of the listener, not so much to bring himself into a genuinely disclosing relation to the things talked of, i.e. to understand them for himself, but rather to understand the talk itself.

This is possible because both the talker and the listener already understand the language in the same average way.

With the omission of going back to the things themselves, whose disclosedness is the soil from which language grows, there is a constant danger that language, solely by virtue of its own potentialities, uproots itself. What is shared is not the primary and immediate disclosure of self and world but an average understanding of the talk itself. Everyday being-together moves largely in a mutual talking-together and in repeating and handing on what has been said. In the course of this the talk loses, or has perhaps never gained, a genuinely disclosing relation to being and beings. The unique gift of speech, "of gifts the most dangerous" (Hölderlin), can itself become the medium for uprooting man from his primary understanding of existence and his nearness to things.

Speech has thus always the possibility of becoming what Heidegger calls *Gerede*, a word for which we have many approximations, none of which hit the target clean in the center. Chatter, gossip, idle talk, groundless talk, bottomless talk, hearsay, all hover on the circumference. Hearsay, although it is not a translation of *Gerede*, can perhaps best convey what Heidegger means: the kind of talk which hears, i.e. understands what is said, and passes on (says on) what has been learned by hearing without "getting to the bottom" of what the talk is about. Writing, as a mode of communicating speech, can bring a further uprooting into everyday existence. Like genuine talk, so genuine writing can degenerate into a bottomless scribbling (*Geschreibe*), which is not so much a "hearsay" as a "read-say," feeding itself on what has already been written and passing it on as a supposed contribution toward keeping the disclosedness of world open. "The average understanding of the reader," Heidegger remarks, "will *never be able* to decide what has been originally drawn and wrung from things, and what is merely repeated." (Cf. SZ, p. 169.)

Groundless hearsay thus helps to "publish" an average explanation of existence and world in everyday being-together. It offers the possibility of understanding everything without going into anything. It develops an average understandability to which nothing remains hidden, so that it in advance hinders and closes a deeper and more genuine approach to things. It is in itself a disguising and covering-over, although, as Heidegger emphatically points out, there is no intention in it to deceive or falsify. Hearsay, simply by omitting to discover things in themselves, is a falsification of speech in the genuine sense, whose whole function is to be dis-covering, i.e. to be true, according to Heidegger's interpretation of truth, as we shall see in a later chapter.

All of us grow up in and draw our first understanding of things from the average explanation of being and beings "published" by everyday hearsay. Much that is useful is learned from hearsay, the common basis on which, and from which, and against which, all genuine understanding and communicating and rediscovering take place. No man can ever keep himself "untouched and unseduced" by the explanations made public in hearsay. (Cf. SZ, p. 169.) It decides in advance even thc possibilities of attunement, i.e. of the basic way in which man lets the world touch him, concern him. "They" have always already prescribed what one sees and how one feels about the world and oneself.

In everyday being-together, whose openness is essentially constituted by hearsay, man's existence is cut off from its primary relations to itself, to fellow-existences and to the world. Its roots are slackened and it sways uncannily in its hold on the disclosedness of self and world (*Schwebe*). Yet, even the uncanniness of this swaying is hidden by the self-assurance and bland matter-of-courseness of an everyday understanding. (Cf. SZ, p. 170.)

b) THE EVERYDAY WAY OF SEEING: CURIOSITY

Among the different ways of "seeing," i.e. of understanding, by which our specific "cares" are guided, we have come across two: care-for others is guided by a considerate looking-back on thrownness, and a forbearing looking-to the self (*Rücksicht* and *Nachsicht*), while everyday taking-care of things is guided by circumspect for-sight (*Umsicht*). The latter, as we have seen, can modify itself to a theoretical only-looking-at things. In everyday being-together, however, circumspect for-sight has another possibility of modification or, perhaps it would be more correct to say, of degeneration. Just as genuine talk can degenerate into hearsay, so the circumspect for-sight of everyday care can degenerate into idle curiosity. This is called by Heidegger *Neugier*, an expressive word in common use, which literally means greed for the new. This curiosity is in the strictest sense of the word "idle," because it arises when everyday existence has nothing more at hand which needs to be taken care of. The care of circumspect for-sight to discover and bring near the handy things to be attended to now detaches itself from its proper task and becomes the care of looking around, merely for the sake of looking.

The idleness of curiosity must on no account be confused with the leisureliness of a theoretical "only-looking," which stays with things in order to understand them, and which, in the highest sense, is an admiring gazing on beings in their pure essence. The curiosity of circumspect for-sight which has broken free of its proper boundaries is exactly the opposite. It roams far and wide out into the world, not in order to understand things but simply to see how they look. In this greed for novelty lies the care of everyday existence to provide itself constantly with new possibilities of delivering itself over to the world.

As against the leisureliness of a "theoretical" staying with things, the idleness of curiosity is characterized by a constant jumping off from the new to the still newer. Curiosity is a not-lingering with things, which gives itself always fresh opportunities for scattering and distracting itself and leads to a new uprooting of man's being as being-in. It will be remembered that "being-in" means dwelling-in . . . , staying-close-to . . . , in-habiting . . . a world familiar to us in this or that way. The not-staying and self-scattering of curiosity drives man's being-in to a loss of dwelling (*Aufenthaltslosigkeit*).

Groundless hearsay and roaming curiosity are not merely two different ways of everyday being-together, but one drags the other with it. They decide together what one must have seen and heard. Hearsay leaves nothing unexplained, curiosity nothing undiscovered, and so they offer to everyday existence the guarantee for a supposed genuineness and vitality of "living." This supposition brings to light a third phenomenon which constitutes the public disclosedness of everydayness. (Cf. SZ, p. 173.)

c) AMBIGUITY

The ambiguity which characterizes everyday being-together spreads not only over the explanation of world and of the things within it but, most importantly, over the possibilities of one's own existence together with other existences. It is not only that the all-knowingness of hearsay and curiosity makes it impossible to distinguish what is genuinely known from what is not, but it also publishes in advance what is to happen and what can and will be achieved. The broadcasting in advance of what can be done is usually a good enough reason not to throw oneself into the necessarily slow business of actually carrying it out. Supposing someone does carry out something, then the ambiguity of hearsay and curiosity has already taken care that the achievement, the moment it is finally realized, looks already obsolete. The ambiguous "fore-knowing" and "fore-seeing" of all possibilities make out that the action and the actual achievement are something belated and secondary. Consequently, people are as a rule misguided as to what are, and what are not, the genuine possibilities of their factual existence.

The ambiguous openness (disclosedness) of being-in-the-world spreads itself over the way in which people are together in their everyday business and social intercourse. This has often the character of a tense and secretive watching and questioning of one another. "An against-each-other plays under the mask of a for-each-other." (Cf. SZ, p. 175.) But Heidegger immediately goes on to add that the ambiguity does not spring from an intention to deceive, nor is it primarily produced by the insincerity of individuals; it lies already in a thrown being-together in a world.

The three constitutive characters of public disclosedness, hearsay, curiosity and ambiguity, show an ontological connection with each other which points to a basic mode of man's being. This is analyzed by Heidegger just before the opening of the sixth and last chapter of Division One. The place of this analysis, which is entitled "Falling and Thrownness," already indicates its methodological importance to the whole first division of *Sein und Zeit*, providing, as it will turn out, the basis for the exposition of man's being as care.

4. *Falling and thrownness*

The phenomena of hearsay, curiosity and ambiguity have brought into view a peculiar "movement" in man's being, which is called by Heidegger *Verfallen*. This concept has so far been usually alluded to in this book as *fallenness*, in order to avoid presenting the reader with a puzzle until the time came when it could be explained. Now it is becoming evident that what Heidegger means by this concept is not a fallen state of man, fallen perhaps from a state of grace into corruption, but means the *movement* of falling. This movement, moreover, is not one of the accidents that can befall man in his factual existence but is one of the basic ways in which man can-be-in-the-world: in the way of disowning himself. This event cannot be explained as the result of external causes and circumstances but only as a *positive* possibility of being-in-the-world, which in its finite freedom *can* move away from itself, *can* disown the utmost illumination of which it is capable.

But if being-in-the-world essentially tends to "move away," to "err away" from itself, and this cannot be ascribed to any extraneous causes, then the temptation to "err" must lie in the very structure of being-in-the-world itself. Indeed, as Heidegger proceeds to show (cf. SZ, p. 177), the temptation is there already in the fore-throw structure of understanding. Its specific function, it will be remembered, is to bring before and toward itself the whole of the possibilities of being, to which being-with-others-in-the-world essentially belongs. Accordingly, understanding constantly throws out before and toward itself possibilities of being-with "them" in the way of groundless hearsay and boundless curiosity. Purely and simply by its own fore-throw of possibilities, understanding constantly tempts itself to stray away, it literally seduces itself (leads itself off) to seek its own fulfillment in the explanations of self and world made public by "them." Being-in-the-world, as essentially constituted by understanding, is thus in itself "seductive" (*versucherisch*).

But why does understanding seduce itself to seek its possibilities among "them"? Because "their" self-assured all-knowingness reassures it of the fullest and most genuine possibility of being-in-the-world. The care of understanding, which in its own nature is a looking-out for possibilities, is thus offered the calm reassurance (*Beruhigung*) that "they" hold the secret of the true life, i.e. of one's ownmost possibility for being-in-the-world.

The calm of this reassurance, however, does not bring being-in-the-world to a haven of peace, but, on the contrary, it increases the impetus of the fall. Tempting itself to err away from its own genuine possibilities, which can become transparent only in a single self, understanding tends to uproot itself further and further, until it becomes estranged from itself (*Entfremdung*). Among the many possible concretizations of self-estrangement, some of which are especially acutely felt in our own age, Heidegger singles out as an example the opinion that ". . . the understanding of the most alien cultures and their 'synthesis' with one's own will lead to the final and true clarity of man about himself. Many-sided curiosity and a restless knowing-all pretend to a universal understanding of man's existence. . . . In this reassured, 'all-comprehending' comparison of everything with itself, man's existence rushes toward an estrangement in which its ownmost ability for being remains hidden." (Cf. SZ, p. 178.)

This estrangement, however, as Heidegger emphasizes, does not mean that man is "in fact" torn away from himself, but, on the contrary, he is driven into the extremest self-analysis and self-interpretations of all kinds, in which he finally "catches" himself, i.e. becomes completely caught and entangled in himself (*Verfängnis*). But far from genuinely *finding* himself in this entanglement, it finally *closes* all possibilities for an understanding which springs genuinely from his own self. In this seductively reassuring, estrangingly entangling way of being-in-the-world, man so to speak casts his moorings and plunges away from himself, not to fall into some abyss which is not himself but to fall into the disowned way of being himself (*Absturz*).

The movement in man's own being constantly drags him away from the fore-throw of genuine possibilities and drags him into the opinion that "they" dispose of the fullness of life. The constant "dragging away from . . ." and "dragging toward and into . . ." finally reveals the movement of falling as a whirl (*Wirbel*).

The steps of Heidegger's analysis, briefly summarized in the preceding paragraphs, have so far clearly followed from the initial step, namely from the fore-throw of possibilities, whereby understanding constantly leads itself astray. But now Heidegger proceeds to take a new step whose connection with what has gone before is not at all evident and seems even to contradict it. The whirling movement of the fall, Heidegger says, characterizes not only the existential constitution of being-in-the-world but at the same time makes manifest the "throw" of thrownness. Man's thrownness is never a finished fact, which happens once at birth and is then left behind: as long as a man factually exists, he "remains in the throw," which whirls him away into disownment to "them." (Cf. SZ, p. 179.)

But how is it, we ask ourselves, that the "falling," which was first explained from the fore-throw of understanding, suddenly turns out to arise from the "throw" of thrownness? How do these two hang together? Presumably, the connection would be clear if we understood exactly what Heidegger means by saying that man "remains in the throw," but this suggestive phrase fails to convey any precise meaning at the moment. Or is it perhaps wrong to take it for granted that the phrase *must* have a precise meaning? Should it not be regarded rather as a figure of speech, suggestive, and inevitably blurred at the edges? This would go against all that we have come to know of Heidegger's thought, a thought which is incomparably strict and translucently clear, provided, of course, that the grave difficulties of penetrating to it are overcome, and even more, that the clarity proper to an inquiry into being is not expected to be of the same kind as the clarity proper to a mathematical theorem or to a report of a football match. On the basis of what our previous discussions have shown, we can confidently expect that man "remains in the throw" in a strict and precisely understandable sense which will come to light when all that is most basic to Heidegger's thought has been brought into view. Much of it still remains to be discovered. The next chapter, while it cannot take us the whole way, will take us an important step nearer to clarifying the connection between the fore-throw of understanding and the throw of thrownness.

⁂ V The Basic Mood of Dread and the Being of Man as Care

1. *The disclosure of being through dread*

Heidegger's analysis of "falling," as the disowned way of being-in-the-world, brings him to the climax of Division One. Its last chapter has the central task of elucidating the originally whole structure of man's being as care. The extraordinary difficulty of this task will be best appreciated by those readers who have already grappled with the full text of *Sein und Zeit*, for only its most basic themes could be touched upon in this book. The complexity of man's being, as it is brought to light by Heidegger in Division One, is truly overwhelming. It is not surprising, therefore, when Heidegger announces that in order to penetrate to the phenomenon of care, an approach to man must be found through which his being will become accessible in a certain *simplified* way. (Cf. SZ, p. 182.) Nor is it surprising that man is to be brought face to face with his being in the mood of dread, for the most original and most far-reaching possibility of disclosure lies in attunement, of which dread will prove to be a pre-eminent mode. What is surprising is that Heidegger should propose to take for the basis of his analysis the *falling,* i.e. the disowned way of being-in-the-world. The proposal to confront man with himself in a way of existing in which he turns *away* from himself seems strange indeed, until the reasons for it are explained by Heidegger. These may be briefly indicated as follows:

Disowned existence, as a movement of "away from . . . ," makes manifest a threat from which man flees. Although the threat is not fully faced, yet it is there, disclosed in the very recoil from it. This threat, as Heidegger's analysis will show, is revealed by dread, on the ground of which man flees from himself into his occupations with things within the world. The preceding inquiry has shown, however, that the flight of disowned existence is not an occasional, isolated act, but a basic way in which man is-in-the-world. This implies that dread also cannot be an occasional, isolated experience, but must constantly tune man and reveal to him a threat to his existence. Dread is the basic mood which lies at the ground of man's being, although it rarely rises to the surface and few of us might recognize it as fully and explicitly experienced by us. Nonetheless, the threat it reveals is attested precisely by man's flight from it, so that the disowned way of existing may very well serve as a basis from which Heidegger's analysis can start.

Heidegger's first concern is to distinguish sharply dread from fear, which is evidently akin to it and yet radically different. Fear as "fear of . . ." always discovers some definite threat approaching from a definite direction in an already disclosed neighborhood. The whereof of fear, the fearsome, has the character of some handy thing, or real thing or another man approaching from the world. But in disowned existence, it is *from himself* that man turns away: the threat cannot come from beings within the world, because it is precisely *to* these that he flees. The threat revealed by dread cannot therefore strike at man from this or that definite direction, from this or that definite thing, but strikes at him solely from himself. It is not beings within the world that dread dreads, but *being-in-the-world as such.*

The whereof of dread, the dreadsome, is being-in-the-world as such. This thesis is put by Heidegger at the head of the main body of his analysis, to be substantiated in detail by what follows. The first step Heidegger takes is to consider the wholly indefinite character of what dread dreads. How does this differ from the definiteness of a fearsome thing discovered by fear? The difference is not one of degree: the dreadsome is totally other than any possible thing can be. It is not as though dread as "dread of . . ." merely left it vague and uncertain what particular things were to be dreaded: dread makes manifest that things *as such* are wholly irrelevant to it. "Nothing that is handy or real within the world can function as that which dread dreads. The relevance-whole of handy things and real things discovered within the world is of no account. It shrivels up and collapses. The world has the character of complete insignificance. Neither this nor that is encountered in dread with which it could have anything to do as threatening." (Cf. SZ, p. 186.)

This short passage from Heidegger's analysis of dread already shows that here we are face to face with something which cannot be fully understood by even the most serious and sustained effort of thinking—naturally so, since the way in which a mood reveals is completely different from any thinking about it. But, if Heidegger is right in saying that a genuine experience of dread is rare, it seems that most of us are doomed not to understand this central piece of the first division of *Sein und Zeit*. Is there not, we ask, some experience common to us which could at least give us a hint of what Heidegger is analyzing here?

Perhaps we could get a hint of it by considering what the things, which Heidegger says "shrivel up" in dread, normally mean to us. They are primarily the useful and indispensable things "by means of which" we can do this and that. But it is not only that we can do this and that with things; they are also primarily what we can do something *about*. No matter how fearsome a thing is, we may not be totally helpless before it; we can at least try to run away or try to do something, as we say, to help.

But the dreadsome must evidently be of a nature we cannot do anything about. Most of us experience in one way or another, at one time or another, the total impotence and helplessness of "I can do nothing to help," in the face of which the things we *can* do something about shrink into utter insignificance and irrelevance.

The unique power of dread lies precisely in bringing things into the mood of total insignificance, and so making manifest that the dreadsome is not a thing, it is not of the character of any beings at all: it is nothing. Consequently, it cannot be found anywhere within the world, it cannot approach from any definite place or direction in a certain neighborhood. The dreadsome is nowhere and nothing. But, as Heidegger goes on to point out, the nowhere and nothing are not mere nothings: in them lies the disclosure of place itself, of world itself.

This passage, it may be said without exaggeration, is a key to Heidegger's whole thought, provided that it is understood precisely and not in a vague, general way. Let us first consider what Heidegger means when he says that the nowhere of dread discloses place itself. In our everyday experience, a place is a definite here and a there where we ourselves and things are at a certain distance and in a definable direction from each other. But in every definite here and there something like a where, or more precisely, whereness, must already be understood. In order to fix the place of a thing "over there" at such and such a distance and in this or that direction from us, we must be able to relate ourselves to it, so to speak, in a "whereish" fashion. What enables us to do so is the disclosure of whereness (place) itself. This happens directly and elementally in the nowhere of dread. The nowhere does not arise from thinking of all possible places together and then negating them: on the contrary, the very indefiniteness of the nowhere brings to light purely the where, or more exactly, the whereness solely by itself. It is only because whereness is always manifest to us that we can and must relate ourselves to the things we meet by giving them a definite *where,* i.e. a place. Far from being a negation of all possible places, the nowhere is the possibility of place: it makes possible the discovery of the place and space that essentially belong to and help to constitute the world.

The world itself is directly revealed in the nothing of dread. This nothing is not an absolute, total nothing, nor is it an absence or negation of all things, but the sheer other to things as such. It is only because we in advance look beyond things to the nothing revealed in dread that things can and must show themselves to us as a whole, *as* things and not nothing. Only from the disclosed *whole* of things can any single thing stand out and show that it stands in itself as the thing it is. The solid, stable standing-in-itself of a tree, a house, a mountain is precisely what we mean when we point to it and say: It really *is* there, it really exists.

Heidegger's interpretation of dread complements his earlier world-analysis. In working out the worldishness of world, Heidegger showed *how* the world is as a coherent reference-whole in which man understands himself among other beings. This understanding is only possible if beings are given the chance to show themselves in their bodily presence, in what is traditionally called their real existence. It is primarily the function of attunement to disclose the presence of beings as a whole. Each mood, it was said earlier, lifts man into the midst of beings, which are always manifest in a certain wholeness. How and why this is so could not be explained earlier, because it is only in his analysis of dread that Heidegger takes up this problem and offers his solution of it. It is the nothing of dread that opens up the horizon from which and against which beings stand out as a whole. Far from being a negation of all things, the nothing is the possibility of things: it gives things the possibility to show themselves as they are in themselves. This possibility, in Heidegger's interpretation, is the world itself.

Hence the world cannot be a thing, a reality that exists independently: the world is only a fundamental way in which man himself exists. When, therefore, dread brings man face to face with the world itself, it brings him directly before his own being as being-in-the-world. What dread dreads, the dreadsome, is *being-in-the-world itself*. (Cf. SZ, p. 187.)

The revelation of man's own being in dread does not happen in a thinking and judging and making propositions about an object to be dreaded, but in the way proper to attunement: dreading itself reveals to man elementally and purely his thrown being-in-the-world.

As a mode of attunement, dread is at the same time "dread for . . . ." This cannot be for a definite possibility of a factual existence, which is threatened by this or that definite thing or event. Any such definite threat is in advance excluded by the nature of dread itself. "What dread dreads for is being-in-the-world itself. In dread, the nearest handy things, and within-worldish beings as such, sink away. The 'world' can offer nothing, any more than the existence of others. Dread thus deprives man of the possibility of understanding himself from the 'world' and from the public explanations (of 'them') in the way of disownment. It throws man back onto his own ability-to-be-in-the-world, for which dread dreads. Dread individuates man into his ownmost being-in-the-world, which, as understanding, essentially throws itself forward into possibilities. With the 'for' of dreading, dread discloses man's factual existence as possible-being, as it can only be from itself, singly in singleness." (Cf. SZ, p. 188.)

The passage just quoted, and what follows immediately after, will prove to be of central importance to the inquiry into the "owned" way of existing to be carried out in Division Two of *Sein und Zeit*. It is dread as "dread for . . . ," as Heidegger points out, which makes manifest to man his *freedom for* being his own self as a possibility. The pre-eminent revealing power of dread lies in bringing man before the finite freedom of his being-in-the-world, as the same being into which he is already thrown and delivered.

With the exposition of the full structure of dread, Heidegger has brought its strange and unique character into view. *What* dread dreads is a thrown being-in-the-world. This has proved to be the same as what dread is *for:* the ability-to-be-in-the-world. But not only that. As Heidegger emphatically points out, the sameness extends even over dreading itself, which, as an attunement, is a fundamental way of being-in-the-world. The sameness of the disclosing with the disclosed would, to our usual way of thinking, appear to be something in the nature of an empty tautology, a "going round in a circle" that can produce no results. Ontologically, however, it is precisely the sameness which is pointed out by Heidegger to be of utmost importance. Dread reveals man's being purely and wholly in itself as a thrown possibility of being-in-the-world. It is true that the function of every mood is to disclose man's being in all its essential articulations, as existence (self), world and being-in (dwelling in . . . , inhabiting . . .). But while other moods refer man to beings other than himself, dread detaches him from them and brings him purely to himself as a single being-in-the-world.

But the uniqueness of this mood, it might be thought, is perhaps only "read into it" by ontological interpretation. To prevent such a suspicion from arising, Heidegger calls to testimony the explanation of dread given by everyday common sense, which, as Heidegger often says, no one would accuse of any hankerings after philosophy. How does everyday experience explain this mood? In dread, it is commonly said, "one feels uncanny." The German word for uncanny, *unheimlich,* literally means *unhomely.* The seriousness of the discussion which Heidegger goes on to devote to this word indicates that what may seem to be merely an afterthought to the analysis of dread will later prove to be its very core. What does Heidegger show as coming to light in this commonly attested feeling of uncanniness?

First, it is the peculiar character of indefiniteness, the nothing and nowhere of the dreadsome which is expressed by the *uncanny.* But at the same time, the uncanny is the *unhomely,* the not-being-at-home. The everyday familiarity with and at-homeness in the world is suddenly broken in dread. The usually taken-for-granted at-homeness comes into the existential mode of not-at-home. This brings into view what it really is *from* which the disowned way of being-in-the-world flees. It flees *from* the uncanny not-at-homeness that lies at the ground of a thrown being-in-the-world. It flees *to* the reassured at-homeness made public in the explanations given by "them." This flight, however, has been shown to be not merely accidental and occasional; it is constant and basic. Ontologically speaking, this means that "the reassured-familiar being-in-the-world is a mode of the uncanny not-at-homeness of man's being, not the other way round. *The not-at-home must be grasped as the more original phenomenon in the existential-ontological sense.*" (Cf. SZ, p. 189.)

In view of the extraordinary power and penetration of Heidegger's analysis of dread, which may absorb the reader's whole attention, it must be stressed that the conclusion just quoted is its most important result for Heidegger's central question: How is it possible for man to understand being? What does being mean? It is already beginning to emerge that the manifestness of the *not* is most fundamental to our understanding of being, and so to our existence as men. The *not*, it now appears, is not originally disclosed by understanding as man's ultimate possibility: it is revealed from the beginning by dread which already tunes all fore-throw of the possibilities of a finite being. Man is not finite because he does not "in fact" last forever. In this sense, a stone or a tree are equally finite, whereas Heidegger means by finiteness the fundamental and unique character of man's being. Man exists finitely because dread in advance reveals to him a *not* in his impotent and uncanny not-at-homeness. This *not* is said to each man alone, and only in hearing it can he understand "that I already am." This understanding, into which a latent dread constantly tunes man, is nothing else than the throw of thrownness. As soon as and as long as a man factually exists, he "remains in the throw."

These reflections, while they do no more than unfold some

of the implications of Heidegger's analysis of dread, do in fact run far ahead of what can come *explicitly* into view at the end of Division One. Our aim is only to understand the basic trend of Heidegger's thought, whereas Heidegger himself has to give the strictest evidence for every step he takes. This makes the unfolding of his main theme necessarily slow and laborious. Even the concept of care which Heidegger is able to work out at the end of Division One is still a provisional concept, showing the ontological structure of only the disowned (falling) way of being-in-the-world. It is, one might say, the "disowned" care of being. Its main articulations into existence (self), thrownness (facticity) and fallenness have already been discussed. (See pp. 50 ff. of this book.) Much of what was then obscure has since become clear. At this stage, therefore, a short discussion of the concept of care will be sufficient for our purpose.

2. *The structure of man's being as care*

In approaching the climax of Heidegger's "Preparatory Analysis," it is helpful to remind ourselves of two points. The first is that the word *man* is only a make-do translation of *Dasein,* giving only the ontic meaning of this essentially two-dimensional, ontic-ontological term. Taken in its primary and most important *ontological* sense, *Dasein* means the disclosed thereness of being. When, therefore, Heidegger says that the being of *Dasein* is care, he does not *only* mean that the original whole of man's being, which we express simply by saying "I am," is to be interpreted as care. He means at the same time, and much more importantly, that being can only be there as care; only as a factually existing being-in-the-world (care) does the illumination of being happen.

This brings us to the second point to remember: if care

is the name for the "actual" thereness of being, it must be the originating source, the gathering place, of any understanding whatever of being. It stands to reason, then, that care must have an extremely complex structure; and this is expressed by Heidegger in the following formula: "ahead-of-itself-already-being-in-(the-world-) as being-near-to (beings encountered within the world)." (Cf. SZ, p. 192.)

Since even this formidable concept of care will later prove to be incomplete, the first point to clarify is what is still missing from it. This can best be done by recalling the idea of being as such, i.e. what- and how-being, something, nothing and notness. As we have seen, the what- and how-being of things, and things as such, (something), are disclosed from the world and are clearly accounted for in the care formula. The mysterious nothing has proved to be the world itself. On the other hand, the notness that most fundamentally determines man's existence cannot yet be made explicit in the present formula. That is why in the course of his further investigations Heidegger will have to complete and reformulate the concept of care in a new way.

Let us now examine the complicated structure with which Heidegger presents us at the end of Division One. It is so unlike any care we have ever experienced that it always remains strange and hard to grasp: ahead-of-itself-already-being-in-(the-world-) as being-near-to (beings encountered within the world.) At first sight, the whole formula looks extremely clumsy and alienates with its abundance of hyphens and its parentheses. More attentively considered, however, it will be seen to gather into itself in the most compact way possible all that Heidegger's inquiry has so far shown to be fundamental to man's being-in-the-world. The "ahead-of-itself" obviously indicates the ontological character of existence. On the ground of the fore-throw of possibilities, man is never merely here and now like a thing, but is constantly out beyond himself, relating himself, in the first place, not to other beings, but to his own ability-to-be. This way of being, in strictly ontological terms, is a being toward an ability-to-be: man constantly relates himself to, bears himself toward, a possibility of his existence in a definite way. Since the care-structure we are considering at present is that of disowned existence, the "self" which care is "ahead of" is always the scattered they-self.

But, it will be remembered, the evidence on which Heidegger is basing this interpretation was gained from the phenomenon of dread. How and where did dread show the "ahead-of-itself" structure of care? In what dread dreads *for,* namely for man's ownmost ability-to-be. At the same time, dread brought elementally into view that the ability-to-be is only possible to a being *already* thrown into a world. The whereof of dread, the dreadsome, showed itself as a thrown being-in-the-world. The "already" expresses the inexorable facticity of thrownness, the impotence to undo the "that I already am." The meaning of the whole phrase, "already-being-in," may be summed up as follows: man dwells in the world in such a way that his own dwelling manifests itself to him always as an already accomplished fact; he can never go behind the "already" to originate his own being.

But, it will be noticed, "the-world" now stands in parentheses. The reason is that care, in the strict sense, is the structure of what would traditionally be called the "real existence" of man, whereas the world is only an existential character of his being. If Heidegger were writing an ontology of the traditional style, the world would function as a category defining man's being.

Similarly, "beings encountered within the world" also stand in parentheses, but for a different reason. These beings are not man himself, nor are they purely ontological structures like the ahead-of, already-being-in and being-near-to. They are concrete, ontic beings that must be distinguished from the strictly ontological concept of care, to which they nevertheless essentially belong: the structure of being-near-to directly refers man to other beings within the world.

It is to these beings that man constantly flees on the ground of a hidden and latent dread. In the concept of care we are considering, the being-near-to (beings encountered within the world) means the fundamentally falling way in which man loses himself in his occupations with things. In this mode of existing, man's being-with others like himself has a predominantly worldish character. Hence the "beings encountered within the world" imply other existences as well as things. It may be noted that the structure of being-with others is not made explicit by Heidegger: it is implied both in the "ahead-of-itself" and in "already-being-in."

But apart from leaving the "being-with" implied, Heidegger's formulation of care shows with unparalleled compactness the disclosure of self, world and beings within the world as it is made possible by the structure of man's being. The philosophical significance of the concept of care is difficult to grasp at a glance. This is one reason why the last chapter of Division One does not close immediately after the exposition of care, but goes on to show how the perennial problems of philosophy gather themselves in man's being as care as the "place" of their origin. In Greek-Western ontology, these problems were posed and their solution attempted on far too narrow a base, leading to such senseless problems as the demand for "proving" the reality of the "external world." But, as Heidegger is now able to show, all disclosure of reality and world is grounded in and made possible by man's being as care, which it is senseless to try to "prove" to itself.

Above all, it is only now that Heidegger can turn to the

most fundamental and central problem of all philosophy, the problem of truth. In the course of Division One, this central problem has been discussed only incidentally, lacking the basis on which it could become the main theme of interpretation. With the exposition of care, the required basis has been gained. Accordingly, Heidegger now turns to give an existential interpretation of truth, which it will be our next task to consider. Strange as this will seem in comparison with the logical theories of truth to which we are accustomed, Heidegger claims that it is no more than the interpretation demanded by the oldest insights into truth which were once alive in our philosophical tradition but now lie buried under logic.

☙ VI Truth, Being and Existence. Heidegger's Existential Interpretation of Truth

The oldest name for truth in Greek-Western philosophy is *aletheia*. For Heidegger, the central meaning of *a-letheia* lies in *lethe*: hiddenness, concealment, coveredness, veiledness. The *a-* has a privative function. The whole word can be faithfully rendered in English by expressions like un-hiddenness, un-concealment, dis-closure, dis-covery, re-velation. Although the elemental Greek experience of truth as a violent and uncanny spoliation, whereby things are wrenched from hiddenness and brought out into the light to show themselves as the things they are, has long since been neutralized and made harmless by theoretical definitions of truth, a reflection of the original insight still lingers in the English words no less than in the Greek *aletheia*.

The sense in which truth is to be understood in *Sein und Zeit* is unhiddenness, disclosure and discovery. This makes it immediately evident that the whole treatise, even when it does not mention the word, is an inquiry into truth—

necessarily so, because truth and being belong together. The disclosure of being that happens in and with man's being as care is the original phenomenon of truth itself. This original truth, often called by Heidegger *ontological* truth, is the condition of the possibility of all *ontic* truth, i.e. of the discovery of beings within the world in various ways and degrees of explicitness and exactness.

According to Heidegger's interpretation, truth is not some reality that hovers over and apart from man but is the fundamental event that happens with man's disclosing way of being. "To be true," for Heidegger, primarily means "to be disclosing," and this is the basic way in which man exists. The truth of owned existence will prove to be the most original phenomenon of truth, but this cannot be shown until the inquiry has been carried a stage further in Division Two. Co-original with the disclosure of man's own being in a world is the discovery of beings within the world. These beings are "true" in a secondary sense: they are not discovering, but discovered, and thus able to show themselves as and for the beings they are. A proposition (judgment) is true insofar as it discovers things, takes them out of hiddenness and lets them be seen in and from themselves. But whereas traditional philosophy has for long regarded the proposition (judgment) as the primary *locus* of truth, Heidegger shows it to be a far-off derivative of original truth, whose "locus" is the existential constitution of man's being as care. The essence of propositional truth has traditionally been thought to lie in the correspondence of cognition (judgment) with the thing cognized. Heidegger does not reject this theory as wrong or false; his aim is to demonstrate its derivative character. (Cf. SZ, pp. 223 ff.; also WW, pp. 7 ff.)

At first sight, it might seem to be a mild kind of criticism of the traditional definition of truth to say merely that it is derivative. But, it must be remembered, Heidegger is not talking about just any kind of study; he is talking of philosophy, whose business is to go to the originative source. In its sphere, any derivation is in itself a de-generation. How is the derivative propositional truth, which Heidegger holds to have usurped a dominant place in philosophy, further elucidated by him?

Propositions, like statements and pronouncements of any kind, are ontic phenomena which belong to language. This, as Heidegger's previous inquiries have shown, requires for its foundation existential speech *(Rede)*, which has been defined as the articulation of understandability. The function of communicating pronouncements is to share the already disclosed being-in, self, world, and beings within the world with the listener and so bring him into a disclosing relation to the things talked about. Among the many possible kinds and modes of pronouncements, the propositions which logical theories of truth have in view are far from being primary. This is interestingly shown by Heidegger in a simple but illuminating example. He compares the everyday pronouncement, "The hammer is too heavy," with the theoretical-physical proposition, "The hammer is heavy." Between these two pronouncements, there is literally a world of difference. In the first, the discoveredness (truth) of the hammer is in advance understood from the workaday world. In the second, the world in which a man lives has disappeared: this massive thing, the hammer, is now only-looked-at from the horizon of the substantiality of substantial bodies, which can be defined, among other things, by mass (weight). (Cf. SZ, Sec. 69b.) The proposition par excellence which traditional logic has in view is of the second type. Its truth is clearly several stages removed from the original discoveredness of things as handy utensils, not to speak of its derivative character insofar as it necessarily rests on existential-ontological foundations which make the discovery of things first of all possible.

The proposition (judgment) can be communicated both in speech and writing, preserved, handed down and handed round. It thus acquires a certain handy reality within the world: it is there when it is needed and relieves us of the trouble to bring ourselves into a primarily disclosing relation to things themselves. It is only now that the possibility of everyday hearsay becomes fully understandable: it lies in the nature of propositions that they preserve the discoveredness (truth) of things and so maintain, albeit in a secondary and derived way, a certain disclosing relation to the things themselves.

As Heidegger's previous analysis has shown, there is a tendency in everyday hearsay to let the handy proposition entirely take over and carry the function of disclosing and discovering, which it does by preserving the "discoveredness of . . ." this and that. So it comes about that when the need arises to demonstrate the truth of something, i.e. when recourse is taken to things themselves to attest that they are such and such, what they are compared with are the propositions whose "property" truth has become. If what the handy proposition says is found to agree with, to correspond with, how the real thing shows itself to be, then the proposition is confirmed as being "really" true. In accordance with the basic trend of traditional ontology, the whole of the relation: "proposition–correspondence with–real thing," is understood to be something "real." The truth, which is thought to be the distinctive "property" of the proposition, itself acquires the character of reality, and its original "locus" in the existential structure of man's being is forgotten.

In Heidegger's interpretation, however, truth cannot exist somewhere by itself like a thing, and cannot have the ontological character of reality. Truth, as disclosing and discovering, can only be when and as long as man factually exists. Understood in this way, it may be said that truth is "relative" to man's being. But does this "relativity" mean that truth is delivered over to the arbitrary invention of a subject and to the fallibility of his thinking? This is far from what Heidegger intends to say. Original truth as the disclosure of being, Heidegger says, a priori determines man's being through and through. His own way of being is the last thing man could ever invent or think out for himself. Truth is anything but the achievement of a subject or a product of his thinking faculties; it is the existential structure of care that is in advance so "organized," so "laid on," as to make man open both to himself and to other beings. If man is able to discover any truth by his own efforts, this is only possible for him because he himself is let into the original happening of truth, for which he is used and needed, and only in being so used and needed is he able to exist as man. (Cf. Ge, pp. 34 ff.) Not man disposes of truth, but rather it is truth that disposes of man.

Just because truth is not the property or invention of man, it in advance assigns to him the way and direction in which disclosing and discovering can proceed. For instance, as we saw earlier, the articulated significance-whole of world (ontological truth) already prescribes definite ways in which the things discoverable within it can "hang together," can "make sense." The predisclosed whole of significance itself directs man toward . . . , refers him to . . . , other beings in certain ways, and so enables man to take his direction from . . . , to keep himself right by . . . , the things themselves that meet him within his world. The discovery of things (ontic truth) is not arbitrary and lawless, because it is in advance directed to bind itself to the things themselves. This is why ontic truth must prove and verify itself in and by the things which it brings to light.

Since, however, all the ways in which man exists are

grounded in his finite freedom, in his disclosing relation to things he *can* omit verification, he *can* refuse to let them show themselves as they are in themselves, he *can* force them into horizons of explanation that are completely alien to them. The seemingly obvious principle that, in an explicit inquiry into any specific kind of beings, the way of approach, the method of investigation and verification, must be drawn from *their* way of being and not from some preconceived notion of scientific truth, is frequently stressed by Heidegger, who is never afraid of saying the "obvious" where it is necessary. In view of the widespread desire today to approximate every explanation to the exactness of mathematics, Heidegger lays emphasis on the following points:

1. The exactness of cognition is not necessarily synonymous with essential truth. For instance, the measurements of time and space in our everyday world are ludicrously inaccurate compared with the scientific measurements of events that happen to substances in an indifferent universal space. (Cf. esp. SZ, Sec. 23.) Nevertheless, statements like, "It's a stone's throw away," or, "You can walk there in half an hour," are definitely understandable and perfectly appropriate to a world inhabited by everyday care. The paths on which a man carefully goes about his business are different every day, but it is precisely in this way that the "real world" is originally discovered and is truly at hand. It is, therefore, not a priori certain that when we have exactly measured, say, the distance of the sun from the earth, and measured the sun itself as a complex of moving particles, we have understood it more truly than when everyday care discovers its handiness for warmth and light, for growth and life.

2. The prevalent tendency to regard the exactness of mathematics as the standard for the *strictness* of scientific truth is vigorously contested by Heidegger. Exactness, he

maintains, is not synonymous with strictness. (Cf. SZ, Sec. 32, esp. p. 153.) Mathematics is not stricter than history, it is only more exact, and it can be so only because the existential foundations relevant to it are much narrower than those required for history. As for philosophy itself, the strictness of thought it demands cannot be approached by any ontic science, yet its findings are in principle not susceptible of the kind of proof and demonstration which are possible to the ontic sciences. Its method and mode of verification, as we shall see in the next chapter on phenomenology, must be drawn from the unique nature of its own subject matter.

Since philosophy concerns itself with being, whose disclosure is truth itself, Heidegger assigns to philosophy the highest place among all explicit, "thematic" inquiries into truth. At the same time, he vigorously insists that no philosophy can in principle claim to be absolute or the only possible one. Like all explanation and interpretation, it is one of the finite possibilities of man's existence, and as such it stands at the same time in truth and in untruth.

As a factually existing being-in-the-world, man stands co-originally in truth and untruth. Just as the disclosing way of existence cannot be of man's own making, so the possibility of hiding, erring and covering over, cannot originally be in man's own power. Man errs, not only and not primarily because his intellect is fallible and he cannot in fact know everything, but because hiddenness and concealment essentially belong to the event of unhiddenness and disclosure. It is paradoxical, and yet understandable, that the most original truth lies precisely in revealing the hidden *as* hidden. It is the recoil from this abyss of truth that sends man back to beings, at the same time whirling him away from himself to the things within his world. Man errs away from himself, not by a conscious or subconscious act of self-deception, nor even aware of a desire to cover over the finiteness of existence, but because it belongs to his thrown and falling way of being. Untruth as hiddenness, erring and covering-over originally belongs together with truth as unhiddenness, disclosure and discovery; the two are one and the same event.

The existential interpretation of truth, Heidegger maintains, is the necessary interpretation of the insight into truth which lies in our oldest philosophical tradition and is expressed in the word *aletheia*. The goddess of truth leads Parmenides before the ways of discovery and concealment, between which the thinker has to choose by understandingly distinguishing the two and deciding for one. This means: man stands co-originally in truth and untruth. The same tradition, moreover, has always brought together truth and being. Parmenides said: *To auto gar noein estin te kai einai.* (Fragm. 5 quoted in SZ, p. 212, and very often in Heidegger's later works.) "The same namely are apprehending and being." Although this oldest insight into the essence of truth begins to be covered over already in Greek philosophy, it reasserts itself at its end with Aristotle, who can still identify truth with being and beings, calling the latter "the unhidden," "the self-showing," "the true."

The logical definitions of truth that later become dominant in Western philosophy also have their roots in Greek thought. The theory of propositional truth is an offspring of the traditional inquiry into beings as beings and has its rightness and validity concerning the definition of the substantial being of things. This truth, however, is not only limited and derivative but is not the most important kind of truth. Far more important to us than a correct cognition of things is the openness or pretense that concerns our own existence, on the basis of which we make our vital decisions and which determines the genuineness of our relations with other men. (Cf. WW, pp. 22 f.)

But it is not enough merely to define the limits of logic and its truth, nor is it enough to go back to an older tradition and revive it. The *aletheia* has not merely to be rediscovered, but has to be more originally understood than was possible at the beginning. (Cf. US, p. 134.) The hiddenness at the heart of the *aletheia,* although elementally experienced, did not become a problem for Greek thought. Attention turned not to the remarkable event that the unhiddenness had happened, but to what had come to light through this event: beings *as* beings. Truth, as a coming to light from concealment, has been thought to belong to being. In Heidegger's interpretation, it is rather the other way round: being belongs to the event of truth, which happens with the existence of man. Truth, being and existence are a single event, to which original untruth, as hiddenness and erring, essentially belongs.

Finally, one point may be raised and briefly considered: the concrete bearing of Heidegger's interpretation of truth on his own inquiry. It has clearly emerged from the preceding discussions that, in a fundamental analysis of man's being, the truth of existence has to be *wrested* from the covering-over which characterizes the everyday and disowned way of existing. Hence the urgency of finding the right approach to man and the proper method whereby the existential analysis can proceed. The importance of the phenomenological method for *Sein und Zeit* is evident on every page. It is no exaggeration on Heidegger's part when he writes that his investigations "have become possible only on the ground that had been laid by Edmund Husserl." (Cf. SZ, p. 38.)

☙§ VII The Concept of Phenomenology *

Husserl's pure or transcendental phenomenology must be sharply distinguished from all other methods or disciplines that bear the same name. In a general sense, phenomenology means the study of the forms in which something appears or manifests itself, in contrast to studies that seek to explain things, say, from their causal relations, or from evolutionary processes, etc. The method of phenomenology is sometimes characterized as "descriptive," but this is considered by Heidegger to be tautologous, since the concept of phenomenology, properly understood, already implies description.

In his "Exposition of the Inquiry into the Meaning of Being" (cf. SZ, Sec. 7), Heidegger gives a preliminary concept of phenomenology, leaving the full concept to be elucidated

* The difficulties of Husserl's thought have already been pointed out. It is a study on its own, and no short description can make its basic principles genuinely understandable, let alone do justice to it. The reader who wishes to go thoroughly into the matter might perhaps best turn to the first volume of Husserl's *Ideen,* one of the few of his works that have been translated into English.

in Division Three. As long as this division is missing from *Sein und Zeit,* Heidegger's discussion of phenomenology remains not only short but also incomplete. It is, moreover, restricted to Heidegger's own aims and needs. His interpretation of phenomenology as primarily a method, which prescribes only *how* an investigation is to be carried out, but not *what* is to be investigated, would be contested by the most distinguished exponents of Husserl's thought, and above all by Husserl himself.

Heidegger introduces his discussion of phenomenology by explaining Husserl's well-known maxim: "*Zu den Sachen selbst!*" "To the things themselves!" The "things" referred to in this maxim, as we shall see presently, are not concrete, material things, but the "phenomena" themselves. The maxim formulates the demand that no time-honored concepts or theories, however well-proven they may seem to be, must be taken over and made the starting point of some constructed evidence. Only phenomena that have been originally brought to light and been directly demonstrated as "self-evident" can satisfy the phenomenological demand for truth and claim to hold a place in the investigation.

After this first, broad characterization of the method, Heidegger proceeds to examine in detail the two components of the concept of phenomenology: phenomenon and *logos.* To begin with, phenomenon is a word that has been used in so many senses both in philosophy and outside it that a strict, unambiguous definition of its meaning has become necessary.

The Greek word *phainomenon* means the manifest, the self-showing. Heidegger defines the basic meaning of phenomenon as "that which shows itself in itself." The Greeks occasionally identified the *phainomena* with *ta onta,* things, beings. There are, however, various ways in which things can show themselves; it is even possible that they show themselves as they are *not,* but only seem to be. Seeming is a self-showing in which things look as if they were such and such, but are not truly so. Seeming is thus a privative modification of phenomenon. Only the positive and original meaning of phenomenon, however, is to be admitted into its definition: that which shows itself in itself.

Both phenomenon in the strict sense and seeming as its privation must be distinguished from other ways in which things can appear. Appearing, appearance, come from *adparere,* to come forward, to show oneself, i.e. originally they mean the same as phenomenon. This is why appearing and appearance *(Erscheinung)* are often used to define phenomenon—a practice that can lead to hopeless confusion in view of the manifold and ambiguous meanings of "appearance." A symptom, for instance, a feverish flush on the patient's face, appears, shows itself, but in so doing it points away from itself to something else, to a disturbance in the organism. The disturbance, the illness, is often said to "appear" in the symptom, and yet the illness does not in the strict sense appear at all, it merely announces itself in and through the symptom. All signs, symptoms, symbols, indications of any kind, in which something announces itself without directly appearing, must be distinguished from phenomena in the strictly defined sense, if hopeless confusion is to be avoided.

The situation is further complicated by yet another sense in which appearance *(Erscheinung)* can be understood. It can mean an emanation of something that itself remains essentially hidden. In this case, appearance means an effect, a product, which indicates a producer, but in such a way that in showing itself it constantly conceals the true being of the producer: it is a "mere appearance." Kant uses the term *Erscheinung* in a twofold sense. In his thought, the word means in the first place simply "the objects of empirical intuition." But these appearing, self-showing objects—phenomena in the original and genuine sense—are at the same time emanations of something that essentially hides itself in them—they are "mere appearances."

Without going into still further complications mentioned by Heidegger, it is abundantly clear that his definition of phenomenon as that which shows itself in itself is both necessary and right. It is, however, as Heidegger immediately points out, only a purely formal concept of phenomenon. The formal concept can be deformalized by determining what are to be taken for phenomena par excellence. One such possible deformalization has already been mentioned with Kant's "objects of empirical intuition." These objects are phenomena in the strict and genuine sense; they satisfy what Heidegger calls the vulgar concept of phenomenon.

The phenomena which phenomenology seeks to bring to light, on the other hand, are of an entirely different order. Before they are concretely defined, however, Heidegger examines the second component of phenomenology, the *logos*. In the history of philosophy, the *logos* has been interpreted in widely different senses, as speech, reason, judgment (proposition), concept, definition, ground, relation. Heidegger renders the *logos* in its basic meaning of speech *(Rede)* but warns that this translation can only justify itself when it has been shown what speech itself means.

Aristotle explains the function of speech as *apophainesdai:* to make manifest that which is spoken of. (Cf. *De interpretatione,* cap. 1–6; Met. Z. 4; Eth. Nic. Z.) The inner connection of phenomenon with *apophainesdai* jumps to the eye. The speaking *phainesdai* lets something be seen, shows something; *apo* . . . , from itself. That is: insofar as the speaking is genuine, it draws what it says from that which is spoken of. Speech is a demonstration, not in the derived sense of reasoning and proving; it demonstrates in the original sense, it points to . . . , it directly lets something be seen. This "demonstrative" way of making manifest, however, is not the character of every form of speech. Begging for something, for instance, also makes manifest, but in a different way.

Since the function of the *logos* as *apophansis* is to show something, it can have the form of a synthesis. But synthesis does not mean a connecting of ideas, a manipulating of psychical events. The "syn" has a purely apophantic meaning: it lets something be seen in its *togetherness with* something, it shows something *as* something.*

The generally accepted view that Aristotle assigns truth to the *logos* (proposition, judgment) as its original locus, Heidegger points out, is quite unjustified, because it overlooks that Aristotle is thinking of the *logos* in contrast to a more original way of discovering, of being true: the *aisthesis* and *noein*. The *aisthesis,* the simple, sensuous perception of beings, always discovers, insofar as it aims at something that is genuinely accessible only through it and for it. Thus, vision always discovers color, hearing discovers sound, etc. In the purest and most original sense true, i.e. always discovering, so that it can never cover over, is the *noein,* the pure "seeing" of beings in their simple essential being. This seeing can never be false, never cover over, although it can remain an un-seeing, inadequate to fulfill its disclosing function.

The possibility of falsehood arises with the synthesis-struc-

* The "as" is not expressed in speech but constitutes the explanation given by what is said. For instance, the proposition, "the hammer is heavy," by defining the hammer in respect of its weight, lets us see it *as* heavy. The *as* which constitutes the explanation given in speaking is called by Heidegger the "apophantic 'as.'" This is to be contrasted with the original *as,* whereby a particular thing comes to our understanding *as* a theater, *as* a bus, in one word, *as* a utensil of a specific character. This original *as* of explanation is called by Heidegger the "hermeneutic 'as.'" (Cf. SZ, Sec. 7 and Sec. 32; the discussion of meaning *(Sinn)* in Part I, Sec.2 of this book is also relevant in this connection. Further, for the meaning of "hermeneutic," see US, pp. 120 ff.)

ture of the *logos*. When the showing of something is no longer simple and direct, but has to take recourse to something else and show the thing *as* something (e.g. the hammer *as* heavy), then a covering-over becomes possible. The propositional truth is only the opposite of this covering-over—a distant offspring of original truth.

The meaning of *logos* has now been sufficiently elucidated for a formal definition of phenomenology. *Logos* says: to let something be seen from itself. Phenomenon says: that which shows itself in itself. Taking the two together, phenomenology means: to let that which shows itself in itself be seen from itself. The concept of phenomenology, Heidegger says, is different from other sciences to which it bears an outward resemblance, such as theology, biology, sociology: the science of God, of life, of human community. These latter name the subject matter that is to be investigated. Phenomenology, on the other hand, only names the way in which the matters to be investigated are to be brought to "show themselves," and this way has already been indicated by the maxim: "To the things themselves!"

But what are the "things" that phenomenology lets us see? What are, for it, the phenomena par excellence? They are *not* the real things we meet within the world, which are always directly accessible to us and do not need a difficult and intricate method to bring them to light. The phenomena of phenomenology must be such that they are usually half-hidden, disguised or forgotten, so that they in themselves demand a special approach. These phenomena are not beings but the being of beings. What phenomenology shows is always "being," its structures and characters, its meaning, its possible modifications and derivations. Phenomenology is the method, the way, in which being, the subject matter of ontology, can be approached and brought to self-showing.

Just because being and its structures are usually half-hidden, or covered over, or disguised, the phenomena have to be *wrested* from the objects of phenomenology. Hence the proper method is needed to secure the starting point of an analysis, the access to the phenomena themselves and the penetration through the prevailing disguises, the most dangerous of which, according to Heidegger, are those ossified concepts within a system which claim to be crystal-clear, self-evident and requiring no further justification.

Since being is always the being of some kind of beings, these beings themselves must first of all be secured in the mode of approach proper to them. This is a preparatory, prephenomenological step which is indispensable for the analysis proper. Here the phenomena in the vulgar sense, the concrete, ontic beings, become relevant. They are the "exemplary beings," the prephenomenological soil for the inquiry whose proper theme is being.

The prephenomenological soil of *Sein und Zeit* is, of course, first and foremost man himself in his concrete existence. But the aim of *Sein und Zeit*, as has been repeatedly said, is not merely to produce a regional ontology of man. Its method is entirely adapted to its own aim as a fundamental (existential) ontology, and is sometimes called "hermeneutic phenomenology" to distinguish it from the same method applied to other philosophical purposes.

Those readers to whom phenomenology has so far been perhaps hardly more than a name will no doubt look for some more detailed explanations from Heidegger as to what his method is and how it works. In the course of unfolding his theme, especially when the inquiry enters into a new phase (e.g. at the beginning of the interpretation of time, Sec. 63), Heidegger does in fact stop to explain in detail the methodological steps about to be taken. Heidegger's elucidations of his method are always important and illuminating, but they do not, of course, aim at giving a simple, overall picture of phenomenology. The broad principles laid down in the "Exposition," on the other hand, are too general to be of much practical help to the reader who does not have at least an elementary knowledge of phenomenology. Such knowledge, although not explicitly demanded by Heidegger, is in fact required to make his treatise fully comprehensible. Without it, the peculiarly phenomenological way of "seeing," whereby such ungraspable phenomena as being and the structures of being are brought to "show themselves," remains a constant puzzle to the reader.

At this point, therefore, we shall turn away from *Sein und Zeit* and attempt to take a few steps toward Husserl's thought. This diversion is necessary not only for a better understanding of phenomenology, but, above all, for indicating the point at which Heidegger radically departs from Husserl. This departure has a profound influence on the style of *Sein und Zeit,* many of whose passages are incomprehensible without some insight into the controversial issues within the phenomenological movement itself.

The divergence between the two thinkers shows itself already in the concept of intentionality, which is the starting point and guiding principle of Husserl's thought. This concept can perhaps be best approached from the formal definition of phenomenon: that which shows itself in itself. Taken by itself, a phenomenon is evidently incomplete: the self-showing needs something to which it can show itself. The "something" which the phenomenon needs as the place of its appearing is thought by Husserl to be transcendental consciousness. This must not be confused with empirical consciousness, which is accessible to us in simple reflection, and which is the sphere studied by the empirical science of psychology. Consciousness

—which must always be understood as transcendental consciousness—is in turn dependent on the phenomenon, since it is its very essence to be consciousness of . . . , i.e. it always goes out for an object, it aims at something, it means something, it intends something. This basic character of consciousness is called by Husserl intentionality. In his thought, especially in later years, "intentional" and "transcendental" tend to become the same. The unique and peculiar character of consciousness is that the phenomena, the objects which it intends, are constituted by its own activities in respect of whatness (essence, "meaning") and in respect of thatness (existence in the traditional sense).

It will be immediately evident to the reader that the disclosure of being which Husserl ascribes to consciousness belongs to the existential way of being in Heidegger's thought. The difference is not a matter of terminology: it is radical, and all the sharper because of the common ground between the two thinkers. Both agree that the metaphysical start from beings is not fundamental enough, and that the home ground of philosophy can only be the transcendental ground where the disclosure of being happens. Further, they are in complete agreement that the "place of the transcendental" cannot be simply one of the realities among other realities in the world, but that the "transcendental subject" must exist in a totally different way from the merely real object. It is at this point that the two thinkers radically diverge. Heidegger strikes out on his own interpretation of the "transcendental subject." Each thinker works out his problem in so different a way that, in spite of many similarities and in spite of Heidegger's incalculable debt to Husserl, a comparison between their thought is difficult to make. Perhaps the best way to indicate the difference is to look a little more closely at Husserl's problem and the way in which he sets out to solve it.

The task of philosophy, as Husserl sees it, is to unfold all the implications that lie enclosed in the intentional structure of consciousness. The first indispensable requirement for accomplishing this task is to develop a reliable method for gaining access to consciousness itself, a method that will enable us to "see" the immensely complicated contents and activities of consciousness just as immediately as we see the "real world" in an act of sense perception.

A sense perception is, of course, itself an act of consciousness. But all our naïve awareness of the real world is already, as it were, an end product of the activities of pure consciousness. These activities lie "anonymously" in all our empirical experience, both of things and of ourselves as the concrete beings we are. Husserl therefore proceeds to suspend, to "put into brackets," to put out of action, everything that we normally accept ready-made from consciousness, and so to turn the phenomenological "eye" to consciousness itself. The method proceeds step by step, by way of a series of "reductions," one of which is called the "phenomenological reduction." In this, the reality of the world, as it is naïvely experienced by us, is suspended, put out of action, not because the reality is in the least doubtful or uncertain but because it is a product of consciousness, and the aim is to get those activities into view which first of all constitute this reality.

What is it, then, that Husserl suspends in the phenomenological reduction? Nothing less than the *is*. But not only the *is* of things is suspended; the *am* must also be put out of action, because what we naïvely experience in the *I am*, is the "empirical subject," the concrete beings we are in the real world. The *am* is no less a ready-made product of transcendental consciousness than the *is* of a thing, and must therefore be neutralized to get the contents of consciousness itself purely into focus.

But, it may be asked, does Husserl intend to say that everything in the world, ourselves included, is a sort of invention, a figment of imagination on the part of consciousness? Any such thought is as alien to Husserl as it is to Heidegger. It is not real beings that are constituted by consciousness, but their *being* in respect of what and how. This achievement of consciousness, moreover, is so little arbitrary that it proceeds by the strictest laws, to discover which is part of the task of phenomenology. Nor does consciousness simply invent the what and how of things but is dependent on receiving the "stuff" (Greek: *hyle*) on which it can go to work. The first problem, indeed, which phenomenology has to solve is how consciousness can receive the "stuff" it needs to be able to work on it.

This problem is much more puzzling than it might seem to be at first sight. Let us consider a real thing, e.g. a red apple. A moment's thought will show that "this red apple" is totally different from "my awareness of this red apple." The real apple is solid, hard, so and so colored, shaped, extended in space, etc. My awareness of the apple, on the contrary, is neither solid, nor hard, nor colored, nor shaped, nor extended in space in any way. It is evident that this real apple, with its real qualities and properties, can never bodily "get into" my consciousness, and yet must be able to present itself to it *as* real, *as* rounded, *as* red, *as* solid, etc. How is this presentation possible?

It is possible through sensations, or sense data (hyletic data), which themselves are of the nature of consciousness and present its activities with the "stuff" it works on. As Husserl's careful and detailed analyses show, these sensations or sense data are already in themselves extremely complex: they are fluid, they shade off, are variable, are surrounded by a courtyard of potential sensations, etc. These manifold and variable sense data, however, would in themselves remain meaningless, if they were not caught up by the so-called noetic (from *nous*) activities of consciousness, which explain their meaning (*Sinn*) by assigning to them the appropriate formal categories, e.g. substance, quality, etc. The noetic activities thus explain the sense data for what they are, e.g. *as* the color of a material thing. In other words, they constitute the whatness, the essence of the object present to, intended by, consciousness. But the "what" already implies being (existence, thatness) of some sort: this is determined by the so-called thetic activities of conciousness, which set the mode of being of the object as, for instance, "certainly there," as well as its time-character, for instance, as "actual, now, present." These manifold and complex activities, in a process of continuous synthesis, bring forth the unified, identical "noema," the "intended," the "meant" object itself in its whatness and thatness. The noema is, of course, not the material thing itself, which could never be "produced" by consciousness; it is the way in which a material thing can be present to consciousness.

Even this oversimplified sketch will certainly suggest to the reader some similarities with Kant, just as Husserl's "reduction" may have reminded him of Descartes' method. To give Husserl's comments on these resemblances in a few words: Descartes was the first to turn toward the sphere of transcendental subjectivity (consciousness), but he got stuck halfway. He did not develop his method nearly radically enough (i.e. he suspended the reality of the world, but not the *I am*). His "thinking subject" remained a merely empirical subject, who exists in exactly the same way as the extended object, so that it is precisely the transcendental achievement of subjectivity that is left unexplained. Kant, on the other hand, penetrated further than perhaps any other thinker into transcendental consciousness but without fully realizing the peculiar nature of the "promised land" he had entered, which he could not therefore fully explore, nor develop the necessary method for its exploration. Kant's great achievement is the achievement of the intuitive leap of genius, which could not complete the arduous, painstaking and enormously extensive tasks involved in a systematic exploration of consciousness.

One of the first tasks of phenomenology must be to analyze all the essential components, structures and functions of consciousness itself. In its first phase, this inquiry has necessarily the character of a so-called static analysis. For the purpose of study, it must bring consciousness, which is essentially a Heraclitean flux, to a standstill. This freezing of a temporal event into immobility, while indispensable, is artificial, and must be complemented by a genetic analysis of consciousness, whose task is to show the generation of its activities in time, and the generation of time itself in consciousness.

This rough sketch of only a small corner of Husserl's phenomenology is all that can be given here without going altogether beyond the bounds set to this discussion. Seen in comparison with Husserl, the parallels in Heidegger's thought are as striking as the differences; it is as if a landslide had occurred, shifting everything onto another plane.

Nevertheless, precisely by striking out on his own interpretation of "transcendental subjectivity," and by adapting phenomenology to the needs of his own question, does Heidegger most strikingly show the potentialities of Husserl's method. The whole of *Sein und Zeit* is a demonstration of phenomenology at work. It strikes the reader at once with its air of vigor and self-reliance, which is in no small measure due to the demand for original experience and self-evidence made by phenomenology. No method, of course, can produce genius, but where the two meet the results are bound to be out of the ordinary. Heidegger can cut through centuries of encrusted and seemingly unchallengeable "truths" by asking one simple question about them. At the same time, as the exposition of Heidegger's basic thought has shown, he is not out to destroy tradition. Heidegger is very far from declaring the whole of metaphysics to have been one vast mistake, arising from an ambiguous use of language. He shows how and why metaphysics had to be as it is, why its language had to be ambiguous, and where the limits of its truth lie. A further, perhaps incidental, but nonetheless delightful result of phenomenological thinking is that it brings alive those technical terms and concepts into which the original insights of past thinkers have hardened, by showing how and from where they had originally been drawn. As to Heidegger's own concepts, they are not abstract generalizations; they explain by making explicit what already shows itself, and the only way to understand them is for each one to see for himself what they are "letting him see." *

* The extraordinary fusion of thought and language, which distinguishes not only *Sein und Zeit* but perhaps even more markedly Heidegger's later works, opens up a topic of great importance and interest. Its discussion, however, would lead too far away from the main theme of this book, and must be regretfully passed over at present.

VIII A Preview of the Tasks and Problems of Division Two

The preceding exposition of Heidegger's leading themes has moved mainly on the level of the "Preparatory Analysis." The difficulties of bringing Division Two into the framework of a general introduction to *Sein und Zeit* have already been mentioned. Not only does Heidegger's inquiry enter into a new phase, but the intricacy of this division calls for a much more closely knit study than has been found to suit the specific aim set to this book. The attempt at a detailed exposition of Division Two can, therefore, be better made in a separate volume. Meantime, a short outline of the course Heidegger's inquiry takes in Division Two and an indication of the answer toward which it strives will be given in the concluding chapters of the present volume. Their aim is not only to give an introductory survey of how Heidegger goes on to develop his main theme but primarily to indicate the perspective in which alone the fundamental ideas and problems raised in Division One can be fully understood.

An extraordinarily important feature of a phenomenological inquiry is its point of departure. How and where does the new phase of *Sein und Zeit* set in? It can only set in at the result achieved by the "Preparatory Analysis": the exposition of man's being as care. The incompleteness of the formulation that Heidegger can give to this concept, on the basis of his preparatory investigations, begins to show itself already on the last page of Division One. The complexity of the care-structure leads Heidegger to ask whether the results so far reached are radical enough. Have they penetrated to the last intelligible ground of the unity and wholeness of man's being? Has the *whole* of man's being been brought into view at all? Evidently not. Being-in-the-world is, after all, ended by death and begun, at the other "end," by birth, whereas the "Preparatory Analysis" has considered only the everyday happening "in between." Moreover, it is the essential character of man that to each one his being is manifest as *mine*. This is the ground of the possibility of owned and disowned existence; but the "Preparatory Analysis" has only brought the average and disowned way of existing into phenomenological view. The incompleteness of the first phase of the inquiry has to be remedied before it can be shown that *time* is the deepest originative ground of the wholeness of man's being as care, and thus the meaning of being as such.

The starting point of Division Two proves to be the question of how the whole man is and how he wholly is. It is the question of the extremest possibilities of man's existence, in contrast to his everyday mode of being. These extreme possibilities appear to lie, on the one hand, in the two "ends" of being-in-the-world which constitute its wholeness, and, on the other hand, in owned existence, constituting the way in which man can be wholly himself, according to his ownmost possibility. The question of wholeness and owned existence, however, is nothing other than the problem of a finitely free being.

But no sooner is this problem formulated than grave difficulties begin to present themselves. In the first place, how can man be a whole at all? Certainly not as a sum, or a thing, or even as a merely-living being is a whole. Man can only be a whole in the way of care, whose essence lies in its disclosing character. The task facing the existential analysis, therefore, is to show whether and how man *can* disclose to himself the whole of his being.

This task, however, seems at first sight to be impossible to accomplish, not for accidental but for essential reasons. We seem to be able to get direct evidence only of the fact of the birth and death of others. As to his own being, a man cannot get behind his own thrownness, he can only find himself already there as a thrown fact; while, at the other end, in experiencing his own death, he already ceases to be.

These peculiar difficulties make necessary a completely different approach to the problem from the one used in Division One. There the existential-ontological problem was approached from the existentiell-ontic basis of the factually existing man; here the method has to be reversed. The first task is to find out whether it is existentially possible for man to be a whole at all, in the way proper to his own being.

This task is completed by Heidegger in a series of detailed and closely integrated analyses, which lead to the conclusion that man cannot be made into a whole by having an end tacked onto his existence in death, but that his being is in itself a being-toward-an-end; as soon as and as long as a man is, he already exists in and from the disclosed possibility of the end of his existence, to which he relates himself in this or that definite way.

How is death, as the disclosed end of man's being, to be

characterized existentially? It is the extreme possibility of the sheer *im*possibility of being-anymore. This possibility can never be transcended by the fore-throw of further possibilities; it is sheerly unrelational, being singly and uniquely each man's own; and it is certain, though indefinite as to the "when." Care thus reveals its ontological character of a being-thrown-into-death, as man's extremest possibility.

This existential-ontological concept of death—so far, it is only a concept—now demands an examination of whether a disclosure of death is ontologically possible. It is possible, as Heidegger proceeds to show, to an understanding which opens itself to a constant threat that rises from the ground of man's being, his thrownness into his "there." This threat is elementally revealed in the basic mood of dread. Understanding runs forward to this threat, fully disclosing it as the extreme possibility of not-being-able-to-be-there-anymore. The disclosure of death is thus seen to be ontologically possible on the basis of attunement (mood) and forward-running understanding.

But all this is, so far, merely an ontological construction and remains worthless unless man himself, in his ontic existence, confirms that the disclosure which has been postulated is possible in concrete experience. Where can such confirmation be found? Heidegger finds it in what is usually called "the voice of conscience." That this "voice" cannot be found as an observable "fact" by an objectively orientated investigation, that its "reality" cannot be proved, does not make it meaningless for the existential inquiry; on the contrary, it shows that in conscience we have a genuine and original existential phenomenon.

The task now is to analyze and interpret existentially the concrete, well-attested experience of conscience. Differently as this may be understood and explained by each man, there is general agreement that it is a voice which has something to say to oneself. It is, therefore, completely in accord with experience when Heidegger sees the ontological function of conscience in disclosing something, in giving something to understand, not to man in general, but to a man singly and individually.

All the stranger is Heidegger's interpretation of conscience as the call of care and of what this call gives man to understand. To mitigate its strangeness, it must be emphasized that Heidegger's interpretation is neither psychological, nor ethical-moral, nor religious, but existential-ontological. Its task is not to find out what circumstances may bring about an experience of conscience, or how its voice is heard and understood by each man, but to show how man must a priori be, i.e. how he must be manifest to himself in his being, so that in his factual existence he *can* hear a voice of conscience at all, and *can* understand himself convicted of a debt (*Schuld*), or summoned to fulfill some obligation he owes.

According to common experience, conscience discloses something like a *debt*. Like the English word, the German *Schuld* has a wide range of meaning: guilt, sin, owing a debt or a duty, being indebted, being responsible for (guilty of) some deficiency or harm. After analyzing the concept of debt, Heidegger comes to the conclusion that a *not* is essentially implied in it. What conscience gives to understand has, in a formal-existential sense, an essential not-character, it is *nichtig*, it is determined by a *not*.

The central problem, therefore, is how this *not* is disclosed to man, so as to make it possible for him to be convicted of a debt or of an owing of any kind. This is only possible, as Heidegger shows, because man is fore-goingly revealed to himself as *owing* his being. He can *never* go behind his thrownness and let himself come, of his own accord, into being. *Not* as thrown by himself but only as a thrown fact can a man ever find himself already there. It is to this *not* that care calls man back from his scatteredness into the they-self and from his lostness to things, giving him to understand that he *owes* it to take over his being and be the impotent (*not*-potent, *not*-determined) ground of an impossibility (the possibility of *not*-being-able-to-be-anymore). Strictly ontologically, man's being as care must be defined as "being the *not*-determined ground of a *not*ness" (*das nichtige Grund-sein einer Nichtigkeit*, cf. SZ, p. 285).

In this new formulation of care, the "being-the-ground," or "ground-being" (*Grund-sein*) comprehends in itself the whole provisional care-structure worked out at the end of Division One. This, however, cannot be shown in detail in the present short preview of Division Two. We must follow up, instead, Heidegger's interpretation of conscience, for, so far, the full phenomenon of conscience has not yet come into view. If conscience is the call of care, then hearing this call essentially belongs to it. And how does man hear this call? Simply by being willing-to-have-conscience (*Gewissen-haben-wollen*), by being willing to be called back to his thrown self and summoned forward to his utmost possibility of not-being. Resolutely disclosed to himself from the ground of his being in the possibility of his end is the way in which man *can* exist wholly as an owned self.

The phenomena of conscience and owing not only provide Heidegger with the required ontic-existentiell basis for his inquiry, but show at the same time that the two, apparently separate, problems of how man can be a whole properly, and how he can exist as an owned self, are one and the same. Existing in the resolute disclosure of his thrown being-toward-an-end is the way in which man can-be-a-whole properly, i.e. in the way appropriate to his own being (*eigentliches Ganzsein-können*).

The exhaustive inquiry into wholeness, end, death and conscience, although it may be regarded as only preparatory to Heidegger's time-interpretation, is important enough to occupy almost exactly half of the more than two hundred pages of Division Two. There is good reason to think that its importance does not become fully explicit in this Division. The phenomenon of conscience and the new formulation of care prepare the ground for finding the answer to the question: How is it possible for man to understand being? Although Heidegger does not expressly say so, the internal evidence compellingly points to the conclusion that here is the basis from which Division Three would have to start.

The immediate function of the long preparatory inquiry, however, is to lead up to the second half of Division Two. What contribution has it made to this most important part of what we have of *Sein und Zeit*? What problem has it solved and what problem has it raised? It has solved the problem of the extreme possibilities of man's being. In so doing, however, it has shown that the structure of care is even more complex than had been suspected, comprehending in itself the phenomena of death, conscience and owing. This increased complexity makes it all the more urgent to lay bare the ontological meaning (*Sinn*) from which the unity of the whole care-structure becomes understandable.

The meaning of care, i.e. the most original and fundamental form of its unity, is *time*. Its exposition needs for its basis the fully unfolded structure of care, because the phenomenon of time can be *originally* experienced only in owned existence. The care of everyday existence is, of course, also grounded in time, but the time that shows itself there is not the original phenomenon but a disowned modification of it.

Heidegger introduces his time-interpretation through the existential structure of death. How is it possible that man can understand himself, whether in an owned or a disowned way, in the utmost possibility of his existence? This is possible only if man is so that he *can* come toward himself in his possibilities at all. The coming, in which man comes toward himself in his ownmost possibility, is the original phenomenon of the future (*Zu-kunft*-coming-toward, or coming-to, cf. SZ, p. 325). But man can only come toward himself in his possibilities insofar as he already is, i.e. *is* as having-been. The original coming-toward himself is thus in itself a coming-back-to the thrown self that man is as having-been. The coming-back-to is the original phenomenon of the "has-been" (*Gewesen*) which springs in a certain way from the future. Coming-toward himself in his possibilities as back-to the thrown self he is as having-been, man is at the same time meeting beings within the world: this is only possible insofar as man is able to *present* them to himself (*gegenwärtigen*). The present is an offspring of the future and past.

The primary ecstasis (standing-out-of-itself) of time is the future. The ecstatic unity of future, past and present, is called by Heidegger timeishness (*Zeitlichkeit*). Timeishness *is* not (i.e. it is not the presentness of a thing), but brings itself to ripeness. It brings itself to ripeness in bringing forth possible modes of itself as time, in the threefold unity of future, past and present. Original time is the time of owned existence which comes toward itself from the *end* that closes all other possibilities. Original time is thus itself closed: it is finite time.

As against the original, finite time of owned existence, how does it stand with the time of everydayness? It is from this existential phenomenon, Heidegger tells us, that the vulgar concept of time is drawn. Losing himself to his world, man understands himself not from his own utmost possibility, but from his makings and doings in company with other people, from the successes and failures he expects or fears. In the first place and for the most part, man comes toward himself in his worldish possibilities. The time that shows itself in this mode of existing is not a man's own, it is the public time, or, more precisely, the published time of the they-self. It belongs to anybody and nobody, that is why it is endless. The traditional concept of time as an in-finite succession of now-points is derived from the disowned time of disowned existence, leveled down and deprived of its ecstatic character, until the original phenomenon becomes well-nigh unrecognizable.

From Heidegger's interpretation of man's being as "existent timeishness" grow the manifold and complex tasks which occupy the second half of Division Two. These require a close study, as indeed does Heidegger's whole time-analysis, of which only the first few steps have been roughly indicated here. Since it is only on its basis that the working out of Heidegger's main theme in the second half of Division Two can be appreciated, no attempt can be made here to give a simple outline of it, such as could be given of the first half of this division. We shall be content, therefore, to summarize briefly the main problems whose solution is assigned by Heidegger to the three long chapters (chaps. 4–6) which compose the second half of Division Two.

The first task facing Heidegger is to show that the wholeness and unity of all the main structures of care, i.e. existence, facticity and falling, are only possible on the ground of man's timeishness. All the essential findings of the "Preparatory Analysis" are once more analyzed and interpreted in terms of time. The timeishness of understanding and attunement, of falling and of the everyday taking care of things, of the fundamental constitution of being-in-the-world and the temporal-horizontal structure of world, and many other themes are worked out by Heidegger in a long chapter entitled "Timeishness and Everydayness" (chap. 4).

The next chapter begins with an analysis of the owned self and its ontological interpretation. This leads to an existential exposition of history from the "happening" of owned existence, illuminating, at the same time, the possibility of a genuine being-with others which springs from one's own self. The problem of the first "end" of man's being, its beginning with birth, which seems to have been unduly neglected in favor of its ultimate end, now reemerges with the important theme of taking over one's thrownness and historical heritage as one's own. While in the context of *Sein und Zeit* the existential interpretation of history stands primarily in the service of Heidegger's fundamental ontology, it has undoubtedly a wider than purely philosophical interest and is considered by many readers as the central piece in Division Two.

In the sixth and final chapter, Heidegger takes up the problem of the vulgar concept of time, the world-time in which things come into being and pass away and the happenings within the world take place. As against the views expounded by some modern philosophers (e.g. Bergson), Heidegger interprets world-time as a perfectly genuine time-phenomenon, grounded in man's everyday being-with others and taking care of things. One of the tasks of this chapter is to show in detail how the concept of a featureless, "unecstatic" time has been derived from the "significant" time of the worldishness of everyday care. Parallel to Division One, where Heidegger sets off his existential interpretation of world against Descartes' "extended world," he now sets off the connection between timeishness, man's factual existence and world-time, against Hegel's interpretation of the relation between time and spirit.

In the last short section of Division Two (Sec. 83), which is the last section of *Sein und Zeit* as we have it at present, Heidegger comes back once more to the central theme of the whole fundamental ontology: the question of the meaning of being as such. Up to the point reached in the inquiry, the question still awaits an answer. The last page of *Sein und Zeit* moves to its close with a series of questions. "How is a disclosing understanding of being at all possible for man?" (Cf. SZ, p. 437.) This question will be answered by laying bare the horizon from which something like being becomes understandable. The original whole of man's existential-ontological constitution is grounded in timeishness. This is where the possibility of an understanding of being must be sought. Heidegger brings the division to an end by asking: "Is there a way that leads from original time to the meaning of being? Does time itself reveal itself as the horizon of being?" (Cf. SZ, p. 438.)

IX Conclusion: An Attempt to Outline Heidegger's Answer to the Question Asked at the Beginning of *Sein und Zeit*

The end of Division Two is designed to throw the interest forward to the answer to be given. It is, therefore, pertinent to ask whether and how far, pending a fully or partly worked out answer from Heidegger himself, it might be possible to discern the answer from what he has already written. No one, of course, would be foolish or presumptuous enough to claim to know in detail what Heidegger would say and how he would say it, but, on the other hand, it would be an unwarranted belittling of his work to aver that nothing can be known of it at all. The solution of Heidegger's problem cannot be arbitrarily tacked on to the first two divisions of *Sein und Zeit* but must rise from them by inner necessity. If the ground has been well and truly laid, the main outlines of the answer must be at least discernible there, especially when some of Heidegger's later works, in which certain hints are made more explicit, are taken into consideration. (Cf. esp. Met, Grund, WW; also some much later works, e.g. US, pp. 213 ff.)

An attempt will, therefore, be made here to outline Heidegger's answer as far as possible. The short sketch to be given will at the same time serve as a concise summary of the most fundamental features of the way in which man exists, as far as they have been discussed in this book.

For a start, we shall consider two questions: First, is there any problem in Heidegger's interpretation of time which is left unsolved? If so, it is reasonable to expect that the explicit working out of this problem will lead to the answer to Heidegger's central question. Second, does Heidegger give us any hint or clue as to where the solution of this problem may be sought?

As to the first question, it may be observed that a problem is implied in the very first step Heidegger takes in his interpretation of time. A disclosure of being-toward-an-end, Heidegger says, is only possible because man exists in such a way that he *can* come toward himself in his possibilities. The whole problem lies in the "can." How is it possible that man *can* come toward himself at all? How and where does this "coming" originate? The answer to this question, we can reasonably assume, will explain the inner possibility of our understanding of being from time, and so the meaning of being as such.

As to the second question, in view of the central methodological importance of dread, it is not an idle guess to say that dread must provide the approach to Heidegger's answer. (Cf. esp. Met, pp. 31 ff.) But if all the ways in which man can be are fundamentally timeish, then the basic mood of dread must have a peculiar and preeminent time-character. Does Heidegger give us any precise indication of this? He does, on page 344 of *Sein und Zeit*: "The possibility of the mightiness, by which the mood of dread is distinguished, shows itself in the peculiar timeishness of dread, in that it is originally grounded in the past, and (only) from it do future and present first of all arise."

Keeping the indications Heidegger gives both in *Sein und Zeit* and elsewhere in view, we shall now attempt to summarize what is most relevant to his answer.

We begin by considering once more the disclosing function of existential understanding. Its remarkable achievement is to fore-throw possibilities. Since being is totally unlike any beings, "to understand being" means something like this: to fore-throw a possibility in which this sheer "other" to any beings somehow reveals itself. This possibility evidently cannot be one among many others, but must be unique and incomparable. What is the unique possibility that reveals itself in man's existence? It is the extreme possibility of the sheer *im*possibility of being-in-the-world-any-more. In this "*im*possible" a *not* is revealed which in advance closes all other possibilities of existence. This *not* belongs to each man alone: it is solely his own being that is at stake, and not another's. The harshness of this *not* is so incomparable and in the strictest sense of the word abysmal that it can only rise from the abyss of man's being, his thrownness into a world. It is the basic mood of dread that originally brings man face to face with the *not* which closes not only the end of his being, but dominates it from the beginning.

What is revealed by dread, however, is not a mere negation, such as we perform in a rational judgment. Dread does not reveal by negating all things, nor by announcing an impending annihilation of the world, but by bringing man's familiar, taken-for-granted being-at-home-in-the-world into the unfamiliar mood of an uncanny not-at-homeness. In the not-canny, not-at-home, the *not* is elementally revealed as a threat that does not come from outside, but rises from being-in-the-world itself.

The way in which dread gives man to understand the *not* is totally different from the way in which he acquires some information about a fact. "In fact," a man may not know about death, its possibility may be kept covered over in the flight of disowned existence, dread may never be fully experienced in a lifetime; nonetheless, as soon as and as long as a man *is*, the *not* is openly or covertly revealed as the extreme possibility in which he already is, and which is singly and uniquely his own.

It is the throw by and recoil from this *not* that throws man into the world and so originates the movement of his being. But what is the world itself into which man is carried by the impetus of the throw? It is revealed by dread as "nothing." The whereof of dread, the dreadsome, it was said, is nowhere and nothing. But it was made clear that the nowhere is not an absence and negation of all places; it is the original disclosure of place itself, of the pure *where* itself.

The world itself, as a fundamental character of man's being, is directly revealed in the nothing of dread. This nothing, however, is not the absence and negation of all things, but the totally "other" to things as such. The incomparable power of dread is to bring man directly before the nothing (world) itself. Face to face with nothing, man is in one leap beyond beings as a whole, among them first and foremost himself. The transcendence of man's being is only possible as this confrontation with the sheer "other" to any beings. What comes to light in this transcendence, however, is not something outside and beyond the world, but precisely beings *as* the beings they are, i.e. in their being. It is the essence of the nothing to repel, to point away from itself, to direct and refer to beings, as totally other than itself. Only in coming to things from the disclosed nothing of world can man understand them in their strangeness: that they are something, and not nothing. (Cf.

Met, pp. 33 ff.) And only in coming to himself from the utmost limit of his being-in-the-world can man understand himself fully as a self existing among other beings.

How is it, then, that man *can* come toward himself at all? The movement originates in the throw by and recoil from the *not* revealed by dread, which throws man into the world and whirls him away to the beings he meets within it. But at the same time, it throws him forward into the extreme possibility of death, in *rebounding* from which he *can* come toward himself in his ownmost possibility. The forethrow not only comes to a limit, but is thrown back by it: it is the rebound that enables man to come toward himself in his possibilities, and so exist primarily from the future.

But it would still remain inexplicable how and why this "coming-toward" should be the primary mode of time, or indeed any time at all, unless the *not* itself had a time-character. If, however, the movement of man's being is the original unity of time as future, past and present, the whole phenomenon of time seems to be accounted for, and it is hard to see what function remains for the *not* to fulfill. Heidegger, however, leaves one possibility open: with the *not* is disclosed *time itself*. As the last sentence of *Sein und Zeit* suggests, it is *time itself* that will reveal itself as the horizon of being. This is the problem with which Division Three would evidently have had to deal first, before the temporal interpretation of the idea of being could have been taken in hand.

In the absence of an explicit answer from Heidegger, do we have any hints from him where we might look for an answer? He gives us a hint in his analysis of conscience. (Cf. esp. SZ, p. 284.) Conscience gives man to understand that he *owes* his being, that he can *never* go behind his thrownness and exist as the ground of his own being. In calling man back to the *not* revealed in his important thrownness, conscience makes manifest the *never*. According to the whole trend of Heidegger's thought, the *never* cannot be a mere negation of time: in it is disclosed the pure *when*, i.e. time itself. If, indeed, man constantly comes toward and back to himself from the *never*, then the whole movement of his being must necessarily have a time-character, or, as one might equally well say, a when-character. And if the *never* is the horizon into which man in advance looks out, it becomes immediately understandable why he must fore-throw all possibilities of being onto time, and why all articulations and modifications of being must have a temporal meaning.

The temporal interpretation of the idea of being as such, the final goal of Division Three, remains for the most part obscure. On the other hand, the way toward this goal is discernible both from the two divisions we have of *Sein und Zeit*, and from Heidegger's later works. Above all, there can be no doubt of his answer to the most basic question: how is it at all possible for man to understand being? The significance-whole of world enables man to understand *that* beings are and *what* they are, i.e. their real existence and their essence. But the unity of the world is itself only possible on the ground of time; and time itself is revealed with the *not* that determines man's existence as a self.

Notness and nothingness (*Nichtigkeit*) are the fundamental existential characters of a finite being. But it must be fully evident by now that when Heidegger speaks of the notness or nothingness of man, he cannot mean what is sometimes understood by these phrases: that man is a null in the world-all, that his being is of no account, or that he comes from nothing and dissolves into nothing and his existence is therefore meaningless and purposeless. Far from declaring man's being to be meaningless because it is finite, Heidegger shows for the first time that an understanding of being, and with it, an understanding of meaning and purpose, is only possible to a finite existence. Man exists finitely, not because he does not in fact last for ever, but because to him a *not* is in advance revealed, and this harsh, inexorable *not* alone has the revelatory power to enable him to understand being and so bring him into the dignity and uniqueness of a finitely free existence.

The disclosure of being calls man to the task of existing as the place of illumination in the world-all. This disclosure, however, cannot happen to some abstract man in general, but only to a single, factually existing man. The circularity of the problem of being has now come fully to light: the manifestness of the *not* makes it possible for man to understand being, but, on the other hand, his own factual self is needed to make manifest the *not*. This is the ground for Heidegger's thesis that ontology cannot be founded upon an "ideal subject," a "pure I," a "consciousness as such," but only upon the factually existing man, because he and he alone, in his own finite existence, is the place of the transcendental.

Glossary and Index

Note: It was found impracticable to cover every occurrence of the most frequently mentioned key words and subjects. Instead, those pages have been listed on which an explanation or an important discussion of the word or subject in question can be found.

GLOSSARY
of German key words and phrases

ABSTÄNDIGKEIT: stand-offishness, 112 ff.
ALLTÄGLICHKEIT: everydayness, 58 f., 116 ff.
ANGÄNGLICH: approachable, touchable, concernible, 79.
ANGST: dread, 25, 32, 127 ff.
AUSRICHTEN: direct, 61.

BEDEUTEN, BEDEUTSAMKEIT: signify, significance, 84 f., 99, 117, 145.
BEFINDLICHKEIT: attunement, 76 ff.
BEI (SEIN-BEI): near-to, close-to, 89 f.
BENOMMEN: enthralled and bemused, taken in, 81.
BESORGEN: taking care, 89 ff.
BESTAND, BESTEHEN: persistence, persist, 20.
BEWANDTNIS: relevance, 101 f.

CHARAKTER (SEINSCHARAKTER): character (of being), 60 ff.

DASEIN, DA-SEIN: man, being-there, thereness, etc., 60 ff., 136.

EIGEN, EIGENST: own, ownmost, most one's own, 45 ff.
EIGENTLICH: owned (existence), properly, 56 ff., 105 ff., 133.
EKSTASE, EKSTATISCH: ecstasis, ecstatic, 50, 171.
ENT-FERNEN, ENT-FERNUNG: un-distancing, 61.
ENTSCHLOSSENHEIT: resolute disclosure, 169.
ENTWELTLICHT: un-worlded, fallen out of the world, 101 f.
ENTWERFEN, ENTWURF: fore-throw, 82 ff.
ERMÖGLICHUNG: possibility, 46.
ERSCHEINUNG: appearance, 152.
ES GEHT UM: it is at stake, it is the issue, 42 ff.
ETWAS: something, 9 ff.
EXISTENZ, EXISTIEREN: existence, exist, 35, 40 ff.
EXISTENZIAL, EXISTENZIALIEN: existential, existentials, 59 ff.
EXISTENZIELL: existentiell, 64 f.

FAKTIZITÄT: facticity, 50 f., 138.
FREIGABE, FREIGEBEN: setting free, to set free, 80.

FÜRSORGE: care-for, 106 ff. *et passim.*

GANZSEINKÖNNEN: can-be-a-whole, 169.
GEGENSTAND: object, 20.
GEGENWÄRTIGEN: to present, 171.
GEGUND: place, neighborhood, 79, 130 f.
GEREDE: hearsay, idle talk, groundless talk, 116 ff. *et passim.*
GEWESEN: has-been, past, 171.
GEWISSEN: conscience, 167 ff.
GEWISSEN-HALBEN-WOLLEN: willing-to-have-conscience, 169.
GEWORFENHEIT: thrownness, 50, 77 ff.
GRUND-SEIN: ground-being, 169.
GRUNDVERFASSUNG: fundamental constitution, 62 f.

IN-DER-WELT-SEIN: being-in-the-world, 70 ff.
INNERWELTLICH: within-worldish, 89.

KATEGORIEN: categories, 60 ff.
KONSTITUTIVE MOMENTE: essential constituents, 60.

MAN, MAN-SELBST: people, "they," "they-self," 111 ff.
MITSEIN: being-with, 81, 104 ff.
MITWELT: with-world, 106.

NACHSEHEN: overlooking (the other self), un-caring toleration, 109.
NACHSICHT: (forbearing) looking-to (the other self), 109.
NEUGIER: curiosity, 120 f.
NICHTIGKEIT: notness, nothingness, 9, 169, 180.
NICHTS: nothing, 9, 130 ff., 178 f.

ÖFFENTLICH, ÖFFENTLICHKEIT: public, published, publicity, public disclosedness, 115, 116 ff.
ONTISCH: ontic, 64.

RÄUMLICH: spaceish, 36, 61, 87 f.
REALITÄT: reality, 41, 63.
REDE: speech, 76, 99, 116 ff., 153 ff.
RÜCKSICHT: (considerate) looking-back (on the other's thrownness), 108 f.

SCHULD: owing, debt, 168 f.
SEIENDE (DAS): beings, things, 14 f.
SEINSVERFASSUNG: ontological constitution, 62 f.
SINN: meaning, sense, 5 ff., 161.
SORGE: care, 49 ff., 136 ff.

STÄNDIGE ANWESENHEIT: standing presentness, 12.
STÄNDIGKEIT: stability, standing, 115.

UM: for, around, 42, 95.
UMGANG: dealings with, going about (for something), 95 ff.
UMSICHT: circumspect for-sight, 95 ff.
UMWELT: the first and nearest world, for-world, 71, 84, 95 ff.
UMWILLEN: for the sake of (for the will of), 42 ff., 84.
UNEIGENTLICH: disowned (existence), not-properly, 56 ff., 123 ff. *et passim.*
UNHEIMLICH: uncanny, unhomely, not-at-home, 134 f.

VERFALLEN: falling (falling captive to the world), 51, 123 ff.
VERSTEHEN, VERSTÄNDNIS: understanding, 27 ff., 82 ff.
VERWEISEN, VERWEISUNG: refer, reference, 61, 70 ff. *et passim.*
VORGÄNGIG: fore-going, 64.
VORHANDENHEIT: reality, substantial reality, 15 f., 99 ff. *et passim.*

WAS- UND WIESEIN: what- and how-being, 9 f.
WELTBILDEND: world-forming, world-imaging, 74 ff.
WELTLICH, WELTLICHKEIT: worldish, worldishness, 36, 70 ff.
WIRBEL: whirl, 125.
WIRKLICHKEIT: reality, 11.

ZEITIGEN (SICH): to bring oneself to ripeness, to arise, 51, 171.
ZEITLICH, ZEITLICHKEIT: timeish, timeishness, 36, 51, 171 f.
ZEUG: utensil, 7 f., 100 ff.
ZUHANDENHEIT: handiness, handy reality, 100 ff.
ZU-KUNFT: coming-toward, future, 171, 176 ff. *et passim.*
ZUNÄCHST UND ZUMEIST: in the first place and for the most part, 57 f.

INDEX

English Translations of Heidegger's Works

Being and Time (Sein und Zeit). Translated by J. Macquarrie and E. Robinson. London: SCM Press, and New York: Harper & Row, 1962.

An Introduction to Metaphysics (Einführung in die Metaphysik). Translated by R. Manheim. New York: Doubleday & Co., 1961.

Kant and the Problem of Metaphysics (Kant und das Problem der Metaphysik). Translated by J. S. Churchill. Bloomington, Ind.: Indiana University Press, 1962.

The Question of Being (Zur Seinsfrage). Translated by W. Kluback and J. T. Wilde. London: Vision Press, and New York: Twayne Publishers, Inc., 1959.

What Is Philosophy? (Was ist das—die Philosophie?). Translated by W. Kluback and J. T. Wilde. London: Vision Press, and New York: Twayne Publishers, Inc., 1958.

In Collections:

Existence and Being. Edited and introduced by Werner Brock. London: Vision Press, and Chicago: Henry Regnery Co., 1949. Containing: *Remembrance of the Poet (Andenken an den Dichter)*. Translated by D. Scott. *Hölderlin and the Essence of Poetry (Hölderlin und das Wesen der Dichtung)*. Translated by D. Scott. *On the Essence of Truth (Vom Wesen der Wahrheit)*. Translated by R. F. C. Hull and A. Crick. *What Is Metaphysics? (Was ist Metaphysik?)*. Translated by R. F. C. Hull and A. Crick.

Existentialism from Dostoevsky to Sartre. Selections by W. Kaufmann. London: Thames & Hudson, and Cleveland: Meridian Books, 1957. Containing: *The Way Back into the Ground of Metaphysics (Rückgang in den Grund der Metaphysik)*. Translated by W. Kaufmann.